A SERIES OF
NEW TESTAMENT
STUDY GUIDES

THE GENERAL LETTERS

HELPS FOR
READING AND UNDERSTANDING
THE MESSAGE

Bob Young

James Kay Publishing

Tulsa, Oklahoma

A Series of New Testament Study Guides
THE GENERAL LETTERS
Helps for Reading and Understanding the Message
ISBN 978-1-943245-22-2

www.bobyoungresources.com

www.jameskaypublishing.com
e-mail: sales@jameskaypublishing.com

© 2018 Bob Young
Cover design by Bob & Jan Young
Author Photo by Jan Young

1.2
All rights reserved.
No part of this book may be reproduced
in any form or by any means
- except for review questions and brief quotations -
without permission in writing from the author.

Table of Contents

Preface to the Series 1

Introduction to the Series 3

A Word About Formatting 9

Brief Introduction to the General Letters 11

Introduction to James 13

James 1 21

James 2 33

James 3 43

James 4 51

James 5 59

Introduction to 1 Peter 71

1 Peter 1 77

1 Peter 2 87

1 Peter 3 97

1 Peter 4 107

1 Peter 5 113

Introduction to 2 Peter 119

2 Peter 1 123

2 Peter 2 131

2 Peter 3 139

Introduction to 1 John 145

1 John 1 155

1 John 2 161

1 John 3 169

1 John 4 177

1 John 5 183

Introduction to 2 John 189

2 John 191

Introduction to 3 John 197

3 John 199

Introduction to Jude 203

Jude 209

Preface to the Series

A number of factors have converged in my life as influences on my method of Bible study and Bible teaching. My undergraduate training in Bible and biblical languages served as the foundation for 25 years of full-time preaching ministry. During those years in ministry, I periodically took graduate coursework in an effort to stay fresh.

When I decided to pursue graduate education diligently, I already loved teaching from an exegetical viewpoint while paying special attention to the historical-cultural context and the grammatical-syntactical features of the biblical text. I had seen the healthy ways in which people respond to thoughtful efforts to explain and apply the message of the Bible. I had developed the habit of using that same kind of Bible study in my sermon preparation. For those reasons, I focused my graduate training in ministry dynamics and how to integrate academic studies with practical applications. Because I did graduate work while continuing full-time work in ministry, I was blessed to have a laboratory to apply and test what I was learning.

My years of teaching and administration in Christian higher education coupled with increased involvement in the world of missions have made me even more aware of the need to view the Bible, insofar as possible, outside one's own social, cultural, experiential, and religious backgrounds. My interpretative efforts today are influenced by my training and experience. I try to understand the biblical context, the historical-cultural context, and the literary context—vocabulary, genres, grammar, and syntax. I try to understand the original message of the author and the purpose of the text as first steps toward understanding the message of the text in today's world. I want to know what the text said and what it meant, so that I can know what it says and what it means today.

As I have prepared these study guides, I have constantly asked myself, "What would I want in a study guide to the biblical text?" I have been guided by this question, at times excluding technical details and academic questions, at other times including such items because of their value in understanding and communicating the text. Above all, I have tried to provide a practical study guide to put in clear relief what the text says as a first step toward valid interpretation of what the text means and how it should be applied today.

I wrote these guides with multiple readers in mind. There is little new in these volumes, but preachers and Bible class teachers will be helped with their study and review of the text. Christians who have an interest in the message of the Bible will be helped by the textual jewels and the summaries that are included. The initial motivation to prepare these volumes came from my desire to provide a resource that will be translated into Spanish, keeping in mind the needs of preachers, Bible teachers, and Christians who do not have access to the many resources and books that exist in English. A good way to describe these guides is that they are simple explanations designed to help with the task of understanding and applying the biblical text. A few technical details are included to help with understanding, to identify repeated words or themes, and to give insights into the message of the text. May God bless you in your desire and your efforts to understand and apply the message of the Bible!

Introduction to the Series

The Purpose of These Guides

To describe the publications included in this series as "Bible study guides" says something about their intended purpose. As guides, these little books do not attempt to answer every question that may arise in your study of the biblical text. They are not commentaries in the strictest sense of the word. The focus of these guides is distinct.

I have as a primary goal to encourage you to do your own study of the Bible. This series of study guides is designed to assist the Bible student with preliminary and basic exegetical work, and to suggest some study methods that will enrich your study and help you identify the message of the text—whether in a specific verse or paragraph, a larger context, or an entire book of the New Testament. A primary goal of these guides is to help you maintain a focus on the purpose and message of the original author. The message of the original writer should inform our understanding of the text and its application today. One should not think that the message and meaning of the text today would be significantly different than the message and meaning of the original document.

The title also says that these guides are "helps." I have tried to provide resources to guide and enrich your study, keeping the purpose of the original author in view. This desire has informed the content of these study guides. Many study guides exist and there is no need to write more books that basically have the same content. Generally, the information included in these guides is designed to help identify the purpose of the original author and the message of the Bible. In some passages, the information included in these guides will provide insights not readily available in other resources.

What Kinds of "Helps" Are Included in These Guides?

These study guides reflect how I organize and understand the text of the Bible, taking into account various exegetical factors such as syntax, grammar, and vocabulary. Along the way, I share some observations that will help clarify passages that are difficult to understand. I have not tried to comment on every passage where potential problems or differences in understanding exist. I have not noted every textual variant in the original text. At times these notes may seem to be unnecessary comments on passages where the meaning is clear; that probably means I am trying to share insights to deepen understanding and appreciation of the text. In other passages, some may ask why I have not included more comments or explanation. Such is the individualized nature of Bible study. The overall goal of my comments is to help maintain a focus on the original author's message and purpose for writing—the "what he said and what he meant" of the original author in the original context.

For each chapter, there is a "Content" section that usually includes a brief outline, followed by notes ("Study Helps") about the biblical text. The content sections of these guides, including how the text is divided and how paragraphs are described, are drawn from my own reading and analysis of the text and from a comparison of several translations. In only a very few cases does the outline provided in this guide vary from the majority opinion, and those cases are noted and the reasons given. In some chapters, there is an overview with introductory comments to help orient the student to the overall content and message of the chapter. In a few chapters, there are some additional observations. Often, a paraphrased summary is included as part of the textual notes or in a separate section after the study helps. As noted above, the comments are not intended to answer every question. In a few cases, I have addressed topics that are not treated in detail in other resources. Texts that are easily understood and matters that are customarily included in other resources are, for the most part, not treated in detail here.

A Useful Tool for Understanding the Message of the Bible

While the primary purpose of these guides is to assist in personal study of the biblical text, these guides will also serve the casual reader who wants to understand the basic message of the Bible. The guides are written in such a way that the reader can understand the general message of the text, along with some interesting and helpful details, simply by reading the guide. One might describe theses guides as a kind of "CliffsNotes" to the Bible, but they are intended as helps and should not be thought of as taking the place of Bible reading and Bible study.

How to Use This Bible Study Guide in Personal Bible Study

This guide is not intended to take the place of your own Bible reading and study but is intended to provide insights and suggestions as you read the Bible, and to be a resource that will help you check your understanding. **You are encouraged to use this guide and your own Bible side by side.** Some sections of this guide may be difficult to understand unless one also reads the specific part of the biblical text that is being described or explained.

No specific translation of the biblical text is included in this guide. Two goals influenced the decision not to include a translation of the biblical text. First, it is hoped that you will be encouraged to use your own study Bible. Second, these notes are designed to be helpful in biblical study regardless of the version the reader may prefer for personal Bible study.

My primary purpose is to make it easier for you the reader and student to analyze and understand the text. Ultimately, you are responsible for your own interpretation of the Bible and you cannot simply follow what a favorite preacher or commentator says. Often the study notes for a chapter or subsection of a chapter are followed by a brief summary of the content, focusing on the message.

<u>Five Steps for Bible Study</u>. The suggested process for effectively using these Bible study guides involves five steps. First, you should read an introduction to the book of the Bible you wish to study. The introductions provided in these guides will serve well. They are for the most part briefer than normal and do not cover every detail. In this series of guides, sometimes one introduction is provided to cover multiple books, as in the case of the Thessalonian correspondence and the Pastoral Letters.

The second step in your study is to read through the book of the Bible you wish to study to understand the overall content. It will be helpful if this can be done at a single sitting. The student facing time constraints may have time for only one reading, but multiple readings will reveal additional details of the book, providing you an opportunity to notice repeated words and phrases and to think about the message of the book, how the book develops its message, and how various parts of the book are connected. You will find help for your reading in the chapter outlines that are provided in these study guides.

Now you are ready to begin your study of individual chapters or sections. The process is simple: read a section of the text until you have a good understanding of it. This is not an in-depth reading to resolve every question but is a general reading to understand the content of the passage.

The fourth step is for you to write your own outline of the chapter or section, with paragraphing that reflects major thought patterns, divisions, and topics. In these study guides, each chapter has a section with suggested paragraphing based on a comparison of various translations. While it is possible to skip this step in which you do your own analysis and paragraphing, and to move directly to the paragraphing provided in the study guide, this is not the recommended approach. You will benefit from taking the time and investing the energy to do this work in initial reading and understanding.

Finally, the study guides have a section of study helps that will help you read and understand the text and keep the intent of the original author in mind as you do more focused study. In many chapters, a final section that summarizes the message of the chapter is included.

Initial Reading and Paragraphing

In other articles and publications, I have explained the importance of preparatory reading and personal study of the biblical text. In the five-step process described above, initial reading and paragraphing occur in the second, third, and fourth steps. When the student carefully works through these steps, it becomes clear that this is a "Bible" study and is not simply a process of reading more background information and commentary from a human author who is trying to explain the Bible. Although many students jump immediately from reading an introduction to reading a commentary, it is important that the student learn to read and study the Bible for herself or himself.

Once the biblical text is familiar, I suggest the student think about the themes that can be identified and how to mark the paragraph divisions, based on the content of the passage and the subjects treated. Once this work is complete, it is good to compare the resulting paragraphing with that of several versions, or with the outlines in the content sections of these guides.

A Note About Paragraphing

Paragraph divisions are the key to understanding and following the original author's message. Most modern translations are divided into paragraphs and provide a summary heading. Ideally, every paragraph has one central topic, truth, or thought. Often, there will be several ways to describe the subject of the paragraph. Only when we understand the original author's message by following his logic and presentation can we truly understand the Bible. Only the original author is inspired—readers must take care not to change or modify the message. A first step toward integrity with the text is to develop the ability to analyze it and establish paragraphs.

Note: This introductory information is not repeated for each chapter. Students will find it helpful to return to this introductory section again and again to guide their study, especially before beginning the study of a new chapter of the Bible.

A Word About Formatting

The format of the Study Helps in each chapter follows the outline that is provided for the chapter. The major points of the outline are used to begin new sections of the Study Helps. Biblical references that introduce sections or subsections of the Study Helps are placed in bold type to assist the student. In the case of paragraphs that cover multiple verses, the biblical references are placed in progressive order on the basis of the first verse in the citation.

Standard abbreviations of biblical books are used. Verse citations that do not include the name of a book (e.g. 2:14) refer to the book being studied. Abbreviations that may not be familiar to some readers include the following: cf. = compare; e.g. = for example; v. = verse; vv. = verses.

The first time a translation is mentioned, the standard abbreviation is included for translations that are less well-known. Subsequent references use only the abbreviation.

Greek words are placed in italics. Often, the corresponding Greek word, a literal meaning, and other translation possibilities are placed in parentheses immediately after an English word. Greek words are written as transliterations in English letters, using the basic lexical form of the word. It is hoped that this will make it easier for the reader without a knowledge of Greek. Many readers will find these references interesting, especially in those passages where there is repeated use of the same Greek word. Readers can quickly pass over this inserted parenthetical information if desired.

In a few cases, parentheses are used to indicate Greek verbal forms or noun forms where this information would be significant to the student with some understanding of grammar. The Greek language uses three classes of conditional statements: clauses that begin with "if." These constructions are noted when the use is significant. The first class condition is assumed to be true from the viewpoint of the author. The second class condition is contrary to fact. The third class condition is hypothetical. Again, the reader can pass over this information rapidly if desired.

The Greek text used is the 27th edition of *Novum Testamentus Graece* which is identical with the 4th revised edition of *The Greek New Testament*.

Quotation marks are often used to call attention to special words or topics, and also to indicate citations or translations of the biblical text, most of which are my own. This is done to help the reader identify references to the biblical text, since no specific translation of the biblical text is included in this Study Guide.

Parentheses are used liberally to enclose information and comments that would often be included in footnotes. It is hoped that readers will find this more convenient, both those who want to read the expanded explanation and those who wish to skip over the parenthetical material.

Comments concerning contemporary applications of the text are limited, but are included from time to time.

Summaries are provided for many chapters, with the goal of helping to make the message of the chapter clearer. Some of these summaries are paraphrases, some are written in first person, from the standpoint of the author; others are written in third person and are explanations of the content. Summaries written in either the first person or third person are not translations and they are not paraphrasing. They are attempts to communicate the basic points and the purpose of the original message.

A Brief Introduction to the General Letters

General Letters is a common description of the seven short letters than immediately follow Hebrews in our English Bibles. These seven letters have only 21 chapters—James has five chapters, 1 Peter has five chapters, 2 Peter has three chapters, 1 John has five chapters, and the books of 2 John, 3 John, and Jude are so brief that they are not divided into chapters. They are usually described as one-chapter books. By volume, the General Letters make up approximately 7% of the New Testament. The designation as General Letters goes back to Eusebius in the third and fourth centuries AD. In his *Ecclesiastical History*, he referred to the letters as "Catholic Letters," with the word catholic meaning "universal."

The designation as General Letters is an apt description in the sense that the letters are not addressed to specific churches or individuals. The exceptions are 2 John and 3 John, both of which appear to be addressed to specific individuals. The book of 1 John does not mention the recipients and does not have the typical characteristics of a first-century letter. Two prominent themes in the General Letters are suffering and heresies.

An interesting aspect of the study of the General Letters is that a number of them were among the disputed books of the New Testament, books whose acceptance into the canon was delayed. Only 1 Peter and 1 John were readily admitted to the New Testament canon.

Much more can be said about the individual books but the best approach is to deal with each book in the specific introductions to the books.

Introduction to James

Overview

For many, James is a favorite New Testament book because of its practical emphasis on Christian living. Luther struggled with the book of James because of its seeming contradiction of the "justification by faith" message in Romans. Luther's description of James as an "epistle of straw" is well-known. Luther's complaint was that he could not find the gospel in the book of James. James was written early; it is chronologically one of the first books of the New Testament.

What literary genre should be assigned to James? The introduction to the book employs a letter form: it identifies the author by name, has a greeting, and refers to the recipients personally as "brothers." However, it lacks other characteristics of a letter: a lack of personal greetings, no specific mention of circumstances, and no closing. Although James has some characteristics of a letter, it is better understood as an ethical instruction that is typical of the genre known as "wisdom literature." The book is an example of New Testament Wisdom Literature; it should be read and understood through that lens.

Even though we cannot specifically identify the situation of the author and the intended recipients, the book of James, as other New Testament books, is nonetheless occasional literature written for specific people in a specific historical context. Our difficulty is that the setting of the book is not easily discerned. It is generally agreed that it was written to Jewish Christians. It bears marks of Jewish influence. What was the overall purpose of the book? Were the recipients facing challenges in living out the Christian faith because of pagan influences? Were there conflicts about physical needs within the Christian community, a community composed mostly of Jews in that time period (cf. Acts 6)? The New Testament speaks about problems of famines at Jerusalem, and most Bible students are familiar with the contribution for the poor Christians in Jerusalem. The idea that James was writing to Christians who were struggling with the responsibility of the Christian community to address the physical needs of its members is bolstered by the internal references to physical needs and economic distinctions (1:2-4, 12; 2:6-7; 5:4-11, 13-14).

James was not recognized as a canonical book, a book that belongs in the New Testament, until late. The book is not included in the Muratorian Fragment, a list of books in the New Testament from the late second century. Eusebius listed it among the disputed books but noted that it was generally accepted. It was not generally received as a part of the New Testament until the fourth century. Providing positive support for its inclusion is the fact that it was alluded to by the Patristics—Ignatius, Polycarp, Justin Martyr, and Irenaeus. It was quoted by Clement of Rome as early as AD 95. It is directly quoted by Origen in the early third century.

Authorship, Date, and Recipients

Author. Authorship of the book is traditionally attributed to James the half-brother of Jesus. This James was a leader in the Jerusalem church (Acts 12:17; 15:13-21; 21:18; Gal. 1:19, 2:12). The approximate dates of the biblical citations that mention this James extend from AD 45 to AD 60. It seems that he became a believer after the resurrection and he was likely among "the brothers of Jesus" who were with the 120 in the Upper Room (Acts 1:14). In Gal. 2:12, he is referred to as a "pillar" in the church at Jerusalem. He is not to be confused with James the Apostle, brother of John, who was killed about AD 44 (Acts 12).

Date. The book should be dated around AD 50. If it preceded the council in Jerusalem (Acts 15, AD 49-50), it is a candidate for the earliest book of the New Testament (along with Galatians, if the perspective of those who support an early date for Galatians is accepted). It is unlikely that the book should be dated later than the early 60s. The early date is supported by the reference to the scattered tribes (1:1), the use of "synagogue" to describe the assembly in 2:2; and by the lack of any mention of Gentile Christians. There is no reference to the controversy over circumcision for the Gentiles; the church appears to be largely Jewish and church leaders are simply teachers (3:1) and elders (5:14). The ideas that James was reacting to Paul's letter to the Romans, or that Christian doctrine was well-established because of the lack of doctrinal references in the book, are not strong arguments in favor a later date.

Recipients. The first verse mentions "the twelve tribes scattered..." This reference is understood as a reference to Jewish Christians, not to non-Christian Jews. The inclusion of James with the General Letters (writings intended for readers in multiple churches) suggests that the book was likely intended for Christians in several different locations (cf. 1 Pet. 1:1-2).

James as Wisdom Literature

An important key to understanding the message of the book of James is its identity as wisdom literature. An entire genre (type) of literature is designated by the description "wisdom literature." If you are familiar with the idea of wisdom literature, you probably think immediately of five books in the Old Testament—Job, Psalms, Proverbs, Ecclesiastes, and Song of Songs. However, wisdom literature is a literary type that is broader than those five Old Testament books, extending even to literature outside the Bible. In the Hebrew Bible, the five books of wisdom are included in "the writings," a division of the Old Testament that includes more than the five books we usually put in that category: add Ruth, Chronicles, Ezra-Nehemiah, Esther, and Lamentations. This statement does not mean that all of the additional books mentioned belong in the category of wisdom literature. But broadly speaking, Old Testament wisdom literature includes sections from other books beyond the five we usually consider.

There are many examples of New Testament Wisdom Literature, including the Sermon on the Mount, the parables, brief sections of various New Testament books, especially the hymns and poetry, and the book of James. Because the breadth and multiple characteristics of wisdom literature are unfamiliar to many, the application of wisdom literature in today's world is often difficult and misunderstood. In this Bible Study Guide, special effort is given to explain the unique dynamics that are part of the process of interpreting and applying wisdom literature.

A "wisdom book" will usually share characteristics and common themes when compared with other wisdom literature. James reflects a knowledge of wisdom literature, both of the five principal books of Old Testament wisdom literature, and of the intertestamental book of Ecclesiasticus (c. 180 BC). This knowledge of the Old Testament is mostly observed in allusions rather than in direct quotations (but see 1:11; 2:8, 11, 23; 4:6).

The writing style of James is similar to Old Testament wisdom writers. James uses many short sentences, he often uses comparisons drawn from nature, he uses questions to teach, he uses proverbs. These literary devices are common in wisdom literature. James also uses diatribe. Diatribe is a strong presentation that is extremely critical of a certain idea. In James's use of diatribe, he sometimes introduces the idea that he will oppose with questions, at other times through a supposed objector.

Other characteristics of wisdom literature include loose structure (lack of outline, many subjects loosely woven together, jumping from one subject to another, repetition of the same subjects), many imperatives (the book of James has 54 imperatives in five fairly short chapters with only 108 verses), and diatribe (questions from a supposed objector, 2:18, 4:13, also compare Ecclesiastes). Some studies compare James with the Sermon on the Mount. One author describes James as two Old Testament genres (wisdom teaching and prophetic teaching) presented in the style of Jesus' teachings in the Sermon on the Mount. Because of the loose structure of the book of James, many efforts to outline the book are almost as long as the book itself. Jewish rabbinical teaching often used multiple subjects ("pearls on a string"), thinking that the style would keep the attention of the hearers.

It is often said that the focus of wisdom literature is practical. If by "practical" one means that the authors of wisdom literature are dealing with real life situations, speaking to people where they are and sharing concrete ideas about how to improve, one may be disappointed. Of course, the book of James is practical in that James is addressing the dynamics and challenges of Christian living. His words are relevant and applications in the lives of contemporary Christians are not difficult to find. But many who call wisdom literature practical are only seeking reinforcement for their own already-established values. Let me summarize it this way: while it may be true that James focuses on how faith is to be lived out, with 1:3-4 serving to introduce the book, in another sense James is thoroughly impractical. As we read and seek to understand James' teachings, we should expect that he will challenge our assumptions, condemn human wisdom, and work from the assumption that change is always difficult and at times impossible. We should find hope in God's powerful presence, even though the worst possibilities of the human dilemma are presented as real possibilities, even for God's people. The way to challenge worldliness in the church is to develop changed thinking—which James describes as wisdom from above—and to focus on the Lord's return.

I like Holloway's summary: if we feel comfortable with the teaching of James then we have probably misunderstood it. It is a radical countercultural message that the church today needs to hear and to follow.

Purpose and Themes of the Book of James

A good way to describe the primary purpose of the book, trying to encompass the various themes and concepts, is that the author was seeking to encourage Jewish Christians who were facing trials, conflicts, and challenges. These problems are reflected in the themes that surface throughout the book. Holloway gives us a simplified list of seven major topics – patience (1:2-4, 12-18; 5:7-12), wisdom (1:5-8; 3:13-18), rich and poor (1:9-11, 2:1-13; 5:1-6), the tongue (1:19, 26; 3:1-12), prayer (1:6-8; 4:1-10), sickness and sin (5:13-20), and faith and works (1:22-27; 2:14-26).

One way to identify the main themes of the book is to develop two lists — a list of the themes that appear most often with multiple repetitions, and a second list of themes that deserve mention even though they are not cited as frequently or are not emphasized as much as those in the first list. Some of the items on the second list may be subpoints of the first list.

The first list must include the following: wisdom (and deception), riches, poverty (and wealth), respect of persons, trials and temptations, God provides, faith, prayer, perseverance and patience, the tongue and speech. While there are many possibilities for the second list, some of the most important are the following: doubt, the temporal nature of life, consistent Christian living, moral purity, righteousness, Christian actions, use of contrasts, attitudes, desires, guidance from the law, God's word, maturity, God's nature, humility (and boasting), judging, and treat others right.

Without doubt some would like to expand these lists, but these two short lists of more than 25 items illustrate the problem — already we have an average of at least five significant themes in each chapter, not including any repetition of the themes. Outlining the book is difficult. Therefore, one of the more popular ways to study James is thematic. Many of the themes mentioned above can be used profitably in the development of classes and sermons.

Content, Organization, and Structure of the Book of James

The content of the book shows an obvious Jewish influence. Parallels have been seen to the five books of Torah, the Old Testament Law, as well as to the Sermon on the Mount. James alludes to Jesus' words and teachings as recorded in the Synoptic Gospels more than any other New Testament book.

Even the casual reader will notice the repeated use of the word "brother" (1:2, 16, 19; 2:1, 5, 14; 3:1, 10, 12; 4:11; 5:7, 9, 10, 12, 19) and the frequent use of the term "Lord" (1:1, 7, 12; 2:1; 4:10, 15; 5:4, 7, 8, 10, 11, 14, 15). Specific mention of "Christ" occurs only in the references to faith in Christ (2:1) and Christ's return (5:8). The use of the vocative term of address, "brothers," may provide a basic outline identifying the introduction of a new topic in the mind of the author, or it may be simply a technique to call attention to especially important matters.

One of the more interesting suggestions for outlining James uses a chiastic structure. Chiasm refers to the Greek letter "chi" which resembles our letter "X." A chiastic outline looks like an arrow, with the major theme in the center. The structure is often described as A-B-C-D-C'-B'-A'. In this example, "D" would be the center point and there would be a correspondence or parallelism between A and A', B and B', and so on.

The chiastic outline of James uses the same form, identifying parallel points as follows.

Temptation and trials, 1:2-27
        Favoritism, 2:1-4
            Rich, 2:5-13
                Faith, 2:14-26
                      Wisdom, 3:1-4:10
                Faith, 4:11-17
            Rich, 5:1-6
        Favoritism, 5:7-12
Temptation and trials, 5:13-20

In five chapters, we have numerous themes and subsections. I have found it helpful to see portions of the first and last chapters as an introduction and conclusion, encompassing three admonition-application sections relating to developing faith, understanding faith's wisdom, and living by faith. Below is a basic overview of that outline. The numbers and letters represent sections of chapters, e.g. 1A is the first part of Chapter One, 1B the second part.)

Introduction	1A-The Christian response to trials and temptations
First Admonition	1B-Listen to God so you can live out the message
Application	2A-Impartiality based on the law of loving neighbor
Second Admonition	2B-Faith is demonstrated by actions
Application	3A-The tongue is a measurement of wisdom
Third Admonition	3B/4A-Wisdom from above when applied seeks God
Application	4B/5A-Live God's wisdom--motives/worldliness/pride/relationships/depend on God
Conclusion	5B—In times of trouble, be patient, persevere, look to God who is substance/stability

Considering the various ways in which the book has been outlined, I state again the fact that wisdom literature is often difficult to outline.

Resources

The Greek text used is the 27th edition of *Novum Testamentus Graece* which is identical with the 4th revised edition of The Greek New Testament. Other tools I find helpful include my Greek concordance (Moulton and Geden), Greek lexicons (Arndt and Gingrich, and some older lexicons), and Greek vocabulary studies (*Theological Dictionary of the New Testament; Dictionary of New Testament Theology*, Colin Brown; and Moulton and Milligan).

Many English translations have been consulted. Those consulted most frequently include the English Standard Version (ESV), New English Translation (NET), and New International Version (NIV).

Various commentaries have been consulted. The studies prepared by Utley reflect my own training about how to approach the biblical text. I appreciate the NICNT; the volume on James was authored by Adamson. Holloway's studies are also helpful.

James 1

[Note: it is suggested that the student read the introductory materials in this guide before beginning any individual preparatory reading and analysis.]

CONTENT

The outline and paragraphing included in the Content section of each chapter are only suggestions or guides. The student is encouraged to identify the paragraphs and subsections within each paragraph to assist in his or her own study. The division of the biblical text into paragraphs is fairly standard in modern translations.

The book of James presents special outlining and paragraphing challenges. In my chapter outlines for the book of James, I try to reflect as many of the principal themes as possible, noting both the introduction and the repetition of various themes. This has resulted in paragraph headings that are often different from those used in most English translations.

Outline of the Chapter
1:1	Salutation and greetings
1:2-4	Faith and joy in the midst of trials
1:5-8	Wisdom and faith help us pray with confidence
1:9-11	Neither poverty nor riches measure life
1:12-18	Testing, trials, temptations and God's gifts
1:19-27	Hear and act on the message of truth, this redefines Christianity

Overview of the Chapter

The primary subject of the chapter relates to the Christian attitude in times of trouble—joy and faith-building in trials, understanding the nature of temptation, recognizing and enjoying God's blessings, living out the message of truth.

An interesting outline of the chapter is built around the characteristics of the faithful Christian. Often, the characteristic is described with a contrast. Consider these descriptions, followed by the textual citation, followed by the opposite concept when such appears in the biblical text. Joy—1:2; wisdom—1:5; faith in prayer—1:6—doubt; glory in Christ—1:9—glory in wealth; persevere in temptation—1:12—yield; quick to hear—1:19—slow to speak; careful in speech—1:19-20; not easily angered—1:19; put off evil—1:21; receive the word—1:21; act on the word—1:22; help the needy—1:27; maintain yourself pure—1:27.

STUDY HELPS

1:1. James is the English version of the common Hebrew name, Jacob. We know that the author of this book was the half-brother of the Lord, but he describes himself as a servant (slave) of the Lord, perhaps because he did not desire to call attention to himself. He writes to "the twelve tribes of the dispersion," referring figuratively to Jewish Christian believers who were scattered by persecution in the early days of Christianity. For descriptions of Christians as the new Israel, compare Rom. 2:28-29; Gal. 6:16; and 1 Pet. 2:5, 9. The typical greeting (*charein*, rejoice, greetings) was often replaced by grace (*charis*) in Christian letters. Here the text has the greeting, *charein*. The various explanations of why James used the typical greeting are only speculation.

1:2-4. Having faith in Christ in the midst of trials causes one to take a different view of life. To see life and its difficulties through the eyes of faith is a choice. This choice is reflected in the aorist middle imperative, "consider" (*hegeomai*, to think, suppose, count). Through the eyes of faith, Christians can see joy in the midst of trials. James often uses the phrase "brothers" or "my brothers" to introduce a new subject. In the book of James, it is not clear whether the reference is to those who share Jewish heritage or to brothers in the Lord. I prefer the latter interpretation. Paul uses the same stylistic technique at times. This may serve to emphasize that the author identifies with the readers. James uses the technique often, perhaps indicating major thought divisions in the book (1:2, 16, 19; 2:1, 5, 14; 3:1, 10, 12; 4:11; 5:7, 9, 10, 12, 19).

Joy (*chara*) is probably placed first in the Greek word order for emphasis. "All joy" may be translated "full joy, greatest joy." The eyes of faith see joy where others see sadness and even hopelessness. Experiencing trials does not bring joy, but faith can see the results of life's trials (*peirasmos*, the process of proving by experience, discipline, or provocation). In the General Letters, Jesus is the supreme biblical example of joy through suffering (1 Pet. 2:21; 3;14-17; 4;12-16; see also Heb. 5:7-9; 12:3-4). Of course, the connection between suffering and glory is also Pauline (citing only a few examples, see Rom. 8:17; 2 Cor. 5:1-7; and Phil. 1:21-29).

Literally, the text says that one "falls into" the trials of life. The verb "to fall" has the preposition '*peri*' prefixed (*peripipto*, aorist subjunctive, literally, to fall around). The aorist subjunctive verb places some degree of doubt. Perhaps not all of the recipients were experiencing severe trials at that particular moment. While we can do things that bring trials into our lives, the thought in these verses is that trials are a normal part of the Christian life and come in many versions (*poikilos*).

1:3. The testing (*dokimion*, cf. 1 Pet. 1:7) of faith produces (*katergazomai*, present indicative, literally, works out or accomplishes, causes, brings to completion) endurance (*hupomone*, constancy, cf. 1:3, 4, 12; 5:11). The present tense verb indicates that developing endurance is a process (cf. Rom. 5:3-4). The testing mentioned was used to prove authenticity, to strengthen, and to approve (cf. 1:12). The reference is to the faith or belief of individual Christians, not to the truth of the body of teachings (the faith, Jude 3).

1:4. The text has an imperative: "Let endurance have a [the] complete work." (Note that I have usually avoided translating *teleios* as perfect.) When the work of endurance is brought to completion (*teleios*), the Christian is brought to maturity (*teleios*, cf. 1:17, 25; 3:2) and completeness (*holokleros*, a word that often relates to health and well-being) with nothing lacking (*leipo*, to leave, thus to be absent, to fail, to lack). Trials in the lives of the recipients have tested and purified faith, worked toward endurance, and produced maturity. While it is not always easy to see this truth, trials can bring blessings and joy to the Christian life. The goal of the Christian life is maturity and integrity with no deficiencies. In the introduction to James, trials are often the result of pressures and troubles.

1:5-8. A common deficiency that keeps Christians from maturity is lack of wisdom. The verb used in v. 4 (*leipo*) is repeated in v. 5. James says in essence, "the goal is to lack nothing, but when you lack...." The first class condition is assumed to be true, thus "when you lack wisdom...." This verse is often read out of context and used to refer to any kind of wisdom for any circumstances that require wisdom. Without doubt, God provides wisdom for living in a world of hurts and difficulties. But in the context, the specific application concerns the ability of the Christian to wisely discern when the presence of trials may be evidence of God's discipline and when the presence of trials is evidence of godly living in a world that stands in opposition to Christianity.

Verse 5 introduces a brief section about prayer (vv. 5-8). God provides wisdom, but Christians are encouraged to identify the need and ask so that they can receive. "Let him ask of God." Ask (*aiteo*, present imperative, suggesting repeated action) is repeated in v. 6, "ask in faith." God's gifts are often received through prayer. Wisdom may be developed from experience, but this text says that wisdom is a gift from God. Some people have lots of experiences and learn little, destined to repeat the same experiences again and again. Wisdom is intellectual, practical, and integrative. One may have the necessary knowledge and not be wise. One may have the necessary experiences and not be wise. Wisdom is the ability to integrate knowledge and life experience.

Confidence in prayer is based on God's nature. God is a giving God (cf. 4:3 where this theme resurfaces). He gives to all generously (*haplos*, literally, without dividing the gift, thus bountifully, liberally) and without reproaching (*oneidezo*). Based on the root meaning of singleness or being undivided, *haplos* (*haplotes*) also came to mean sincere, genuine, and pure.

1:6. "Let him ask in faith doubting nothing." Faith and doubt are contrasted. Faith is essential to receive God's gifts. God hears the prayers of faith (cf. 4:1-3). "Doubting" (*diakrino*, present participle, to judge or discern; but in consideration of the result, hesitating, wavering) is repeated: "the one doubting." (See 2:4 for the same verb, *diakrino*, discerning with the purpose of making distinctions.) In 1:6, doubting refers to being unsettled, tossed by external forces, continually struggling in thought or loyalty.

1:7-8. The doubter (literally, that man) should not expect to receive God's blessings because he is double-minded (*dipsuchos*, literally, two-souled, cf. 4:8) and unstable (*akatastatos*, not constant, inconsistent). The meaning is clear, the message more difficult. In the context, the message seems to be that the wisdom, maturity and deliverance that God wishes to give cannot come to those whose doubts give them "double personalities" spiritually so that they are constantly undecided about their thoughts and loyalties.

1:9-11. The Greek conjunction (*de*) suggests that this paragraph connects with the previous one. A casual reading may fail to identify the connection. The subject of trials, introduced in v. 2, will be taken up again in v. 12. The reference to God's gifts connects 1:5-8 and 1:9-11. A logical question is this: if God is the one who gives gifts, wisdom, maturity, certainty, and other blessings (see 1:12, 17-18), how does one explain that some Christians have possessions and power in this world while other Christians have little? How does one explain wealth and poverty when God is a giving God?

What is the message of these verses? Some brothers live in humble situations. The contrast with the wealthy suggests that the reference is to a brother who is poor. A brother who begins in poverty and is raised up by God may glory (*kauchaomai*) in his improvement and success because it is from God. Or, perhaps the reference is to his exalted status as a Christian, against which background the importance of worldly trials fades. On the other hand, a rich brother is to glory in his humbling. The exact comparison is not easy to discern. Given the theme of the book, contrasting poor and wealthy believers, these verses may serve to introduce the contrast. Everyone needs both a sense of humility (dependence on God) and a sense of worth (value based in God).

One of the best ways to summarize the passage is this: life is not to be measured by worldly wealth and prestige. God gives spiritual gifts that have much more importance than worldly possessions. Everything about this world, including our presence in it, is fleeting. It may appear that the rich are insulated from the problems of this world, but everything and everyone in this world will pass away. For parallels to the withering flower and grass, see Isa. 40:6-8 and 1 Pet. 1:24-25.

1:12-18. In v. 2, the believer falls into trials (*peirasmos*). In v. 12, the believer is blessed by enduring and persevering in trials (*peirasmos*). Despite the fact that various English translations use two different words in these verses, the word is the same in the original Greek. The one who perseveres in maturity and faith will be approved (*dokimos*, see v. 3, testing with the goal of proving what is genuine in order to approve it or exclude it), after which he will receive the crown of life. This crown is likely the same crown as "the crown of righteousness" (2 Tim. 4:8), "the crown of glory" (1 Pet. 5:4), and the "imperishable crown" (1 Cor. 9:25). Verse 12 obviously continues the theme of the giving God who is faithful to his promises.

"Blessed" is a common theme in wisdom literature, both in the Old Testament (with many examples in Psalms and Proverbs) as well as in the Beatitudes of the Sermon on the Mount in Matthew 5.

1:13. The imperative of this verse ("Let no one say") may suggest that some were making a false claim and that they should stop. However, the impersonal imperative may also function as diatribe. Literally, the reading says, "may no one being tried (*peirazo*, to examine or prove) say I am being tried (*peirazo*) by God." The noun form of this verb is used in 1:2 and 1:12. The experiences of this world, including the presence of trials and the possibility of our negative response to life's problems, are not God's fault.

Some have tried to distinguish outward trials in v. 2 from inward or spiritual trials in v. 12. Others have distinguished trials and temptations, seeing in the context of James 1 the use of the same word root with two different meanings. Yet others have noted that some trials are used by Satan to destroy but that God never uses trials to destroy but only to build up. Rather than seeking to build arguments or explanations that depend on drawing fine lines of definition and distinction on the use of the same word in the same context, it is preferable that the student recognize that the author speaks of the fact that trials (*peirasmos*, trials, temptations) are a part of the Christian life and function as testing (*dokimazo*).

The verb *peirazo* is used of the temptation of Jesus in Matthew 4, where temptation is clearly the preferable translation. Temptations and trials do not come from God, neither is God touched by such. God is "untemptable" by evil, and tempts no one. In v. 13 is shown the breadth of the words *peirazo* and *dokimazo*. In *peirazo*, both trials and temptations are present. In *dokimazo*, testing and tempting both exist when one considers both process and outcome.

1:14. Each one is tempted (*peirazo*) by his own desires (*epithumia*) being drawn away (*exelko*) and enticed (*deleazo*, deluded, beguiled). The process is parallel to luring animals into a trap. It serves nothing to place blame for sin—God, the devil, parents, friends, others, my education or lack of it, society, the list of possible causes is virtually endless. Desire (*epithumia*) having conceived gives birth to sin, and sin brings forth (*apokueo*, to bring about by transformation) death. Sin is the result of evil desires and leads to death. The Bible describes spiritual death, physical death, and eternal death. Considering the reference to the crown of life in 1:12, this death is most likely spiritual.

1:16. "Do not be deceived" is a passive imperative. "Brothers," in this verse "beloved brothers," may serve as transition, but the transition is not obvious here. The imperative is idiomatic to introduce a major truth statement (cf. 1 Cor. 6:9; 15:33; Gal. 6:7; 1 John 3:7). Here is the major truth: God gives good gifts, and that truth never varies!

1:17-18. In these verses the concept of the generous, giving God continues. "All generous giving and every perfect or complete gift is from above, coming down from the Father of lights with whom there is no variation or shadow due to changes." Light is a biblical metaphor for good, truth, and holiness. God gives good things. God's light is continuous and unchanging.

1:18. Of his own will, he brought us forth (*apokueo*, to cause to be transformed, see v. 14) by the word of truth, so that we would be a kind of first fruits of his creation. *Apokueo* is not the normal word for giving birth, although the use of the birth metaphor for salvation, becoming God's children by spiritual birth, is well-known in Scripture. Note the parallelism between v. 15 and v. 18, based on the verb *apokueo*. Through desire, sin brings forth death; through truth, God brings us forth to life as the first fruits of creation.

The greatest example of God's giving nature is that he gave us his message of truth whereby we have been transformed to be made over and reidentified as part of his re-creation. Salvation is through the spoken word, but the word must be received. The "word of truth" refers to the gospel in Eph. 1:13, Col. 1:5, and 2 Tim. 2:15. Salvation is not through creation, but through re-creation.

1:19-27. The word of truth that is introduced in v. 18 now becomes the subject. Spiritual transformation is through the word (1:18), the word is implanted and is to be accepted (1:21), the word reveals, as a mirror (1:24), the word is God's law for the new age (1:25). The word is to be heard, accepted, and obeyed (1:19-22). **The need to act upon the word is one of James's major themes.** Hearing and acting upon the word of God redefines every aspect of Christianity.

"My beloved brothers" introduces a new section of thought. The verb is likely imperative although it could be understood as indicative. In this passage, the message of truth is life-changing, first of all because of what we come to know. (In other passages, we understand that our lives are also changed by who we come to know.) The three-step sequence is well-known: quick to hear, slow to speak, slow to wrath. Given the Jewish backgrounds of the book, James may be citing a well-known proverbial phrase (Prov. 10:19; 13:3; 16:32; 17:28; 29:20).

This textual section (vv. 19-27) is an expansion of the sequence of v. 19. The first step is to hear, and not only to hear but to act and obey. The second step addresses speech. The third step addresses anger. Anger is not a sin, but it is a human emotion that often works against the just plans of God and fails to reflect God's righteousness. Angry Christians are seldom effective instruments for communicating God's eternal love.

1:21. "Putting away (*apotithemi*) all filthiness (*rhuparia*) and abundant wickedness, meekly receive the engrafted word which is able to save your souls." We have the ability to decide and are responsible for our decisions. Before Jesus can be "put on" (Gal. 3:27), other things must be "put off" (Eph. 4:22-31; Col. 3:8-14). The overflow of wickedness may refer to that which is "left over." The challenge of rejecting wickedness in our lives cannot be overstated. If the phrase refers to malicious or vicious talk, the reference continues the emphasis on the word.

The instruction to receive the word is another imperative verb. Always the gospel must be received in order to be effective. The truth must be accepted. The process by which the word is received is described as grafting. The word must become a part of us and be lived out. This involves the negative "laying aside" which is often summarized in repentance, and the positive "receiving" which is by faith that hears and obeys. When the powerful word is thus received, the result is the salvation of souls. This salvation is eternal in this passage, although the same word is used in the New Testament to refer to physical deliverance or healing (see 2:14; 4:12; 5:15, 20).

(This is not the place to share an extended study of the use of "soul" and "spirit" in the New Testament, but it should at least be noted that these are ways of speaking about the whole person, often serving as synonyms that are used to designate the entire person. The desire to subdivide the human being into three parts that can be addressed and studied individually is an exercise in futility.)

1:22. Those who hear the word and do not practice it deceive themselves (*paralogizomai*, to misreckon, thus the middle reflexive form means to deceive or delude oneself; occurring elsewhere in the New Testament only in Col. 2:4). Here again is a central theme in James: faith in Christ results in a Christian lifestyle characterized by certain actions and attitudes. The word James uses for "listeners" was used of those who attended classes but never joined the study groups. A modern translation could use the word "auditors." Do not be only an auditor when it comes to studying and understanding the word of God. Hearing is not enough; one must take the tests. One must act on what one knows (2:14-26; see also Matt. 7:21, 24-27). The contemporary church easily falls into self-deception when it defines Christianity too narrowly—measuring Christianity only by church attendance, only by compassion, or only by some other activity.

1:23. The first class condition is assumed to be true. That is, there were some to whom James was writing who were hearing and not doing. Today some Christians attend Bible classes and listen to sermons, but that does not change their daily lives. One author called this practical atheism—the irrelevancy of God. Christianity is not defined by a building or a belief system. Christianity is defined by obedience—hearing and practicing the word in its entirety.

A person who hears and does not obey is compared to one who sees oneself in a mirror. To look at oneself is to see one's "face of birth." While some ancient mirrors provided only distorted reflections (1 Cor. 13:12), God's word functions as a perfect mirror revealing exactly one's true nature. When one uses the word of God correctly, there is no room for self-deception.

1:24-25. A person, beholding himself (*katanoeo*) in a mirror, after having looked (*katanoeo*) goes away and immediately forgets what he saw. He forgets of what kind he was. But one who looks (*parakupto*, gazes intently, closely examines) to the complete law of liberty and continues (*parameno*, stays near, perseveres) in it will be blessed in his actions, because he is not a forgetful listener but an active doer. The complete or perfect law of liberty is parallel to the royal law (2:8). The blessing is promised based on close and constant examination of the word, perseverance, and action. Believers must maintain a close relationship with the word of God, the gospel. Christians must use the gospel to evaluate themselves.

1:26-27. The first class condition is true from the point of view of the author. If someone thinks she is worshipful (*threskos*) based on religious ceremony or piety, or certain rules and rituals that govern daily life, or certain actions, and if that person lives a life unbridled in speech, whatever she does that she considers worship (*threskeia*) is empty and useless. The adjective (*threskos*) and the noun (*threskeia*) are rare in Greek. *Threskeia* is in the LXX only in the Apocrypha. The only other occurrences of *threskeia* in the New Testament are in Acts 26:5 and Col. 2:18, neither with reference to Christian worship. The focus is on how scrupulous one is in one's response to the gods.

Evaluating one's life on the basis of scrupulously participating in ceremony and ritual is self-deception. The constant temptation in Christianity is to substitute the performance of certain actions—Sunday worship, various benevolent activities, evangelism, whatever—for genuine Christian living that answers to every commandment of the word of truth. It is not hard to fit ourselves into the category—sincere and unfruitful Christians who depend on their own checklist to prove they are acceptable.

Remember that the word of God and consistent speech are primary foci in this extended section of James. One must speak right, one must do right. It is not enough to believe right, one must also act. James mentions both aspects of correct action, based on the traditional Jewish definition—love God and love neighbor.

In this early Christian writing, pure religion was sometimes defined in terms of pleasing the God and Father, not in terms of Jesus as Lord (but see 2:1). For the recipients of the book of James, a major problem was apparently how they treated one another based on class distinctions of wealth and poverty (1:8-9; 2:1-4; et.al.) The Jewish backgrounds of James may cause us to remember Micah 6:6-8 where religion is defined as righteousness, kindness, and humility in one's relationship with God. In parallel, James's definition of religion (*threskeia*, worship) involves proper treatment of those who were social outcasts and socially vulnerable (kindness), and the maintenance of one's relationship with God (humility and righteousness). It was not the intention of Micah, nor is it the intention of James, to give a complete definition that addresses every possible element of the godly life. Life with God is expressed in vertical relationship (maintain one's love for God, righteousness) and horizontal relationships (maintain one's love for neighbor, kindness). It would be fair to say that "love neighbor" and "love God" are the two elements mentioned by James, although in reverse order from Jesus' response to the lawyer in Matt. 22:40 and the parallel texts.

To keep oneself unstained (*aspilos*, without spot) from the world is a present infinitive. This phrase refers to purity of life. Summarizing these verses, faith as it is described by James has two aspects—healthy, caring, respectful interpersonal relationships with others, especially with those who are rejected and ignored within the society; and a loving walk with God. These two dynamics may be based on Jesus' description of the greatest and second greatest commandments.

James 2

[Note: it is suggested that the student read the introductory materials in this guide before beginning individual preparatory reading and analysis.]

CONTENT
The outline and paragraphing included in the Content section of each chapter are only suggestions or guides. The student is encouraged to identify the paragraphs and subsections within each paragraph to assist in his or her own study. The division of this chapter into paragraphs is fairly standard in modern translations.

Outline of the Chapter
2:1-13   Warning against partiality, respect for the poor and needy
2:14-26   Faith and works

Overview of the Chapter
     James 2:1-13 continues the discussion of the relationship between the poor and the rich in the church (1:9-11), and builds on the mention of the disenfranchised at the end of the previous chapter (1:27). The teachings of 1:26-27 continue into Chapter 2. In the Old Testament, wealth was a sign of God's blessings (see Leviticus 26, Deuteronomy 27). The early church, composed mostly of Jews, had to balance this concept with the realities of poverty in a culture where approximately 80% of the population was slaves. The paragraph develops a contrast between current practices in the church and the values reflected by the royal law.
     The teachings of James 2:14-26 are straightforward but have nonetheless caused much theological controversy. Many modern-day controversies are the result of doctrinal presuppositions and modern tendencies toward proof-texted theology. The passage will be explored thoroughly in the Study Helps. Suffice it to say here that James does not contradict Paul. The

contradictions that have been seen are the result of failing to understand the purpose, recipients, and context of the books of Romans and James. James encourages active faith as the source of assurance before God. For James, assurance does not come from doctrinal correctness but from a faithful lifestyle that is built on correct understanding. Faith is measured by service. Christians are called to use their resources in kingdom pursuits.

STUDY HELPS

2:1-7. "My brothers" may indicate a new paragraph or new thought (1:2, 1:9). Do not have (*echo*, present imperative) the faith of our glorious Lord Jesus Christ with partiality (*prosopolepsia*, lifting the face, the word occurs only four times in the New Testament). The present imperative with the negative particle often means to stop doing something. Some translations use a rhetorical question to translate the imperative. The point is that God does not show partiality (Acts 10:34; Rom. 2:11; Gal. 2:6; Eph. 6:9; 1 Pet. 1:17); neither should God's people.

Faith (literally, the faith) does not refer to doctrine, as is often the case when the word is used with the article. Here the meaning is belief, a meaning consistent with the use of the word throughout this chapter. The word "Lord" followed by the genitive phrase "of the glory" can be translated "glorious Lord." Lord was often a title for deity; glory reminds of the Shekinah glory associated with Yahweh in the Old Testament. These references are significant — remember that James is a book with a strong Jewish flavor. Divine characteristics are attributed to Jesus.

That James, the physical brother of Jesus, refers to Jesus in such terms without mentioning the physical kinship is often noted. Perhaps James is wanting not to call attention to himself. Jesus was recognized by the church as Messiah and Lord, with divine characteristics. There are few references to Jesus in the book of James.

2:2-4. The third class condition, indicating potential action, is a hypothetical example of how partiality can be shown. Wealthy persons with fine apparel, when they come into the assembly (literally, synagogue, either the Christian worship assembly or perhaps a judicial court setting), are given special attention and good seats. It appears that the wealthy may well be visitors, not members of the assembly (see 2:7). Poor persons in shabby clothes, perhaps beggars, are placed on the periphery of the assembly and given minimal attention.

The early Christian worship assemblies were often fashioned after the synagogue (a word that literally means leading or bringing together). This occurrence of "synagogue" in this passage is the only New Testament use of the word referring to a Christian assembly, most probably reflecting the early date of the book. A related word (same root, but with a prefix) appears in Heb. 10:25. The use here seems intentional since James uses the word "church" in 5:14. The Jewish synagogue was a place of worship and was also a place of judgment and litigation. Some think the assembly described here is not worship but more like a court (Mk. 13:9; Lk. 21:12). If so, the two visitors are litigants in a legal proceeding (see 2:6).

The two distinct treatments, based on wealth and poverty, are evidence of partiality or favoritism. The Jewish historical background would be the mistreatment of the poor throughout much of the history of the Jews, reflected in several of the Old Testament prophets. Are you not discriminating (*diakrino*) among yourselves? Do you not become judges with evil reasonings (*dialogismos*, see Rom. 14:1 for another use of this word)? The questions demand an affirmative response. *Dialogismos* means thoughts, motives, internal considerations of the heart.

2:5-7. The phrase, "my beloved brothers," adds an adjective to the more common usage, "brothers" or "my brothers." This use may connect the author with the recipients. The imperative, "listen," expresses urgency or demands attention.

God chose the poor of the world to be rich in faith and heirs of the kingdom which he promised to the ones loving him (cf. 1:12). The question demands an affirmative answer. Those who are poor in terms of possessions in the physical world are God's elect when it comes to spiritual riches of faith. The poor, often social outcasts, have been chosen and accepted by God as heirs of the kingdom. (In 2:5 is the only use of the word "kingdom" in James.) Here is an obvious contrast to the discrimination and partiality that was honoring wealthy persons above poor persons. Jesus came to preach the gospel to the poor

(Lk. 4:18, cf. Isa. 61). Jesus embraced the poor and they gladly followed him. On the other hand, the rich often rejected Jesus, and Jesus condemned them for their priorities, their misplaced focus, and their lack of faith. The passage should not be used for reverse discrimination. The message is not that all poor persons are saved. Nor is the message that all rich people are to be rejected. The message is that all persons of faith are accepted by God, without worldly distinctions based on possessions.

In dishonoring the poor, the readers have forgotten that the rich are often oppressive, that they themselves (the recipients) have been brought before the courts by the rich, and that the rich are blasphemers of Jesus. In my judgment, these are not descriptions of believers (see 2:2 above) but of visitors.

2:8-13. Two first class conditional sentences introduce this subsection. In Greek, the first class condition indicates that the sentence is true from the author's perspective. First, one does well when one fulfills the royal law to love neighbor as self. The phrase, "according to Scripture," means according to the Old Testament citation. Second, one commits sin and is judged by the law as a lawbreaker when one shows partiality.

2:8. The law was mentioned in 1:25, "the perfect law of liberty" (see also 2:12). The context of James 2 obviously points back to the Old Testament (2:11). The quotation in 2:8 is from Lev. 19:18 (note the teaching in Lev. 19:15 against partiality). This passage was cited by Jesus in Matt. 22:40. In the Sermon on the Mount, Jesus exalted the law, spoke against misunderstandings and misinterpretations of the law, and said he came to fulfill the law.

2:9. Showing partiality is sinful. Such was strong teaching in the context of the early church. Even more, the partiality condemned here was not in ignorance but was willful. The Old Testament law prohibited partiality. Partiality contradicts the royal law, which some have called the "law of love." The Old Testament is cited as authority in this text. Those who show partiality are convicted by the law as lawbreakers. Remember that the New Testament as we know it did not exist when James wrote. James is certainly one of the earliest of the New Testament books, and may be the first one written. The appeal is to the Old Testament which would have been the Scriptures of the early church (see 2 Tim. 3:15).

2:10-11. From his statement that the law defines sin and convicts lawbreakers, James quickly points out that perfect law-keeping is impossible. One little stumble brings guilt, even if one has kept all of the rest of the law perfectly. James, as Paul in Romans 3 and Galatians 3, clearly sees the impossibility of perfect obedience making it possible that righteousness could be claimed meritoriously. Verse 11 is simply an illustration of the point in v. 10. The order of the Ten Commandments in v. 11 reflects the Septuagint (LXX). This Greek version of the Old Testament was in wide use among the Jews and is frequently quoted by New Testament authors, reminding us of the influences of Judaism in the book of James.

2:12-13. James returns to his focus on word and work, talk and walk. Consistency is essential for those who will be judged by the law of liberty. Other New Testament texts make clear that all will be judged (e.g., Acts 17:31; Rom. 14:10; 2 Cor. 5:10). That the early church saw the coming judgment through the eyes of the Old Testament, the "Bible" that they were using, should not be troubling when one considers the context of James.

Two misunderstandings are to be avoided. This text does not contradict Paul's later teaching about the covenants (Galatians 3-4) where he clearly shows that the limited purpose of the old covenant was being fulfilled so that faith in Christ could come to bring us to God. Nor does this text contradict the author of Hebrews in the clear teachings concerning the replacement of the old covenant with the new covenant (Hebrews 7-10). When the text of James is read, studied and understood in context, it does not stand against the clear teaching of other passages concerning the new covenant of Christ. Studied in context, neither does the text of James suggest that the Old Testament covenant is binding forever and will always be the basis of judgment.

God's principles are true. The merciful receive mercy, so that mercy is greater than judgment and is victorious over (literally, boasts against, exults over) judgment. Since all have sinned, God's mercy must win out over his judgment if anyone is to be accepted. But do not be deceived by his mercy, for his judgment will be merciless to those who show no mercy.

In summary, the passage in 2:8-13 is not about meritorious acceptance by God but is a call to fulfill the royal law without partiality and to be merciful to others, doing our best to avoid sin (cf. 1:22-27).

2:14-26. The second part of the chapter presents the contrast and interaction of faith and works. After the passage is explained, a brief summary is provided to help with understanding the message and the application.

2:14-17. "My brothers" introduces a new paragraph. The third class condition is hypothetical, "someone may say...." What is the gain if one claims to have faith but does not have works? Is that faith able to save him? The rhetorical questions anticipate the answer—such is useless, there is no benefit. One can already see the conclusion: faith without works is not a saving faith. In v. 14 and in v. 18 we have examples of James's use of diatribe, the use of a supposed opponent whose thinking is condemned.

2:15-16. James presents a possible scenario. A brother or sister (both words are in the Greek text) lives without sufficient clothing and in constant need of daily food. The example is extreme, the response is equally extreme. To such a brother or sister, if someone of you says, "Depart in peace, keep yourself warm and satisfied," without giving them the basic necessities of the body, what is the gain? The words spoken are perhaps prayerful, but no action accompanies the prayer. It is the promise to pray but there is no follow-up. Such words can hardly be sincere. Verse 16 closes with the same three-word phrase that began v. 14. The phrase serves parenthetically: What gain (*ophelos*, benefit, use, advantage, profit) is there?

2:17. Here is the conclusion. The third class contingency illustrates the difference between hypothetical faith and true faith. "Faith, if it has no works...." The third class condition is necessary because the statement is an impossibility. It is impossible for faith to have no works. Faith is always accompanied by action. However, contemplating the impossibility for a moment, such a faith without actions would be dead because it is alone with itself.

2:18-19. Here is another use of diatribe. Grammatically, these two verses are ambiguous. Fortunately, the ambiguity does not present major problems with understanding the message. The problem concerns the use of pronouns and punctuation in the Greek text. Does the quotation stop at v. 18a, the end of v. 18, or continue to v. 19?

The three options give us four possibilities. (1) Is the someone of v. 18 talking with James, so that there is one opponent questioning the connection between faith and works? In this case, the objector could be claiming that some people have faith while others have works, and that it is unreasonable to expect that one person would have both. The response in 18b is that fruit proves that faith is genuine. (2) Or should all of v. 18 be included in the quotation and be attributed to a supporter? In this case 18a is an objection and 18b is the response of the supporter. (3) Is the passage a conversation between two persons (since "someone will say" is future indicative, not subjunctive). (4) Or does James use the future hypothetically to imagine a possible conversation? Regardless of how one analyzes the verses, the point is clear. Faith is made visible by actions. To claim otherwise is an impossible alternative.

One believing that "God is one" does well (cf. 2:8 for the same wording, "does well"). Is this belief the essence of faith? In Judaism, monotheism (Deut. 6:4-5) was a test of orthodoxy. But in Christianity, mere belief cannot be a sufficient test, because even the demons believe and tremble. Again, the point is the same—mental beliefs must be accompanied by actions to be recognized as genuine "faith." This statement does not say that actions are the sole measurement, for what is believed must also be true. Authentic Christianity encompasses both correct beliefs and corresponding actions.

2:20. Here is the same summary presented in a slightly different form. "Do you want to know...." is more accurately, "Do you want proof or evidence...." The term of address, "empty fellow," may refer to lack of works. Faith without works is useless. There are three possible translations, based on Greek textual variants—dead, useless, empty. Of these, useless is considered "almost certain" in USB⁴.

2:21-22. The first evidence of the connection between faith and works is Abraham. It can be said that Abraham was justified by works when he offered Isaac, because his works were evidence of his faith. Faith was working with his works, and out of his works his faith was perfected (*teleioo*, completed, matured). The reference to Abraham as father may reflect that most of the recipients were Jewish Christians. Several years later, Paul will use the same reference to Abraham as father, but with a different emphasis as he declares Abraham the father of the faithful.

The statement of 2:21 concerning Abraham's justification is not a contradiction of Paul in Rom. 4:1-2. Both texts must be understood in their unique contexts with the purposes of the authors in mind. The verb *dikaioo* is capable of a broad meaning— made righteous, declared righteous, shown to be righteous. The context will determine the meaning. Be careful about the tendency of some inexperienced students to accept only one meaning and to impose it on every context. In addition, James and Paul are using the word "works" in different ways. Paul is describing works of the law and the efforts of the Jews to attain righteousness based on works. Said another way, Paul is talking about works that issue forth from law. James is talking about works that issue forth from faith, a point that is clarified in the phrase of 2:22, "faith was working with his works." The word "works" is used eleven times in this paragraph, only three times in the rest of James.

2:23. This verse refers to Gen. 15:6. Paul refers to the same verse in Rom. 4:3 and Gal. 3:6. That Abraham believed God was evident in his willingness to sacrifice Isaac. His faithful response was counted to him as righteousness. He was called the friend of God (cf. 2 Chr. 20:7; Isa. 41:8).

2:24. The conclusion to be reached on the basis of the Abraham narrative is that justification is not possible by faith alone. Justification involves works (action). (Note: because "works" often carries with it preconceived ideas and incorrect perceptions, a good alternative translation is "action.") Genuine faith is always accompanied by works (actions), so that the evidence of justification by faith is something that looks a whole lot like justification by works (based on actions).

2:25. In parallel to the Abraham narrative, Rahab (a Canaanite prostitute from the city of Jericho, Joshua 2) was justified by works, that is, through what she did when she received and hid the messengers and sent them out secretly. Her actions were the result of her belief. That she was justified by works (of faith) is evidence of the presence of faith in her life. The works mentioned are not works of law but works of faith. Works of law are based in a meritorious legal relationship; works of faith are based in the faith relationship (R0m. 4:11).

2:26. James repeats the principal point. Faith without works is dead, just as the body without the spirit is dead. Faith without works hardly deserves to be called faith. It is the faith of demons, it is useless, it is dead.

Here is a helpful summary. 2:14-17, genuine faith is always accompanied by works of faith; faith without works is dead. 2:18-20, faith and works are not two separate options; faith without works is useless. 2:21-26, justification by works is a description of justification by faith; works naturally and normally follow faith, so that faith without works is dead.

Final Reflections on the Chapter

James and Paul do not contradict one another. Sometime around AD 50 James writes to Jewish Christians to motivate them to actions that correspond to faith. Especially in times of trial, it is easier not to make one's Christianity too obvious. Christianity is not defined by what one claims to believe. Christianity is defined by one's actions because faith is always accompanied by works of faith. James is pro-works (of faith) because he is pro-faith. A few years after James, Paul writes to Jews to convince them that righteousness before God is not based on their Jewishness and their ability to keep the law and demonstrate works of law. Paul is anti-works (of law) because he is pro-faith. Paul and James are looking at the same salvation and the same faith, but Paul is looking at the development of faith and James is looking at the results of faith.

James 3

[Note: it is suggested that the student read the introductory materials in this guide before beginning any individual preparatory reading and analysis.]

CONTENT
The outline and paragraphing included in the Content section of each chapter are only suggestions or guides. The student is encouraged to identify the paragraphs and subsections within each paragraph to assist in his or her own study. The division of the biblical text into paragraphs is fairly standard in modern translations.

Outline of the Chapter
3:1-12   The tongue
3:13-18 Two kinds of wisdom

Overview of the Chapter
That James intertwines a number of recurring themes has already been mentioned. One of those themes, the kind of talking that is appropriate for the Christian (1:19, 26; 2:14; 3:1-12; 4:11-12; 5:12), is a major subject in Chapter 3. A person's words are a mirror of the heart (Matt. 12:34). The importance of our words is a common theme in wisdom literature. The tongue can be either a blessing or a curse. The tongue that is guided by heavenly wisdom will bless others. The tongue can be destructive when controlled by evil.

The first part of the chapter specifically mentions teachers. In this passage is the first mention of teachers in the book of James. Based on the context of the first two chapters of the book, perhaps some who were teachers in the church were not living lives consistent with their teachings. One way to connect the two sections of Chapter 3 is to note the application to teachers. Teachers will receive a stricter judgment, they must watch their speech, their lives must reflect their teachings, they must develop proper attitudes. Very early in the history of the church, there were problems with false teachers (e.g., Galatians). Perhaps the problem in James was with unqualified teachers. Today, many churches struggle with the problem of unprepared teachers. Teachers, like all Christians, must seek wisdom (1:5); that wisdom is affirmed by their words, their lifestyle, and their attitudes. Especially in Old Testament wisdom literature, wisdom is always linked with how one lives. Of course, these principles apply to every Christian.

STUDY HELPS
3:1-12. "My brothers" introduces a new paragraph or a new topic. The warning against many being teachers may reflect that many wanted to speak up during the assemblies (cf. 1 Cor. 14:26-40). First century worship assemblies were likely much less structured than what we experience in churches today. Christians leaders must reflect a high standard because they serve as examples for every Christian.

3:1-2. Not many should strive to become teachers. This instruction likely refers to assemblies where many could speak. It does not refer to the spiritual gift of teaching which would be determined by the Spirit and not by the individual. Later, teaching is associated with the leaders who are described as pastor-teachers (Eph. 4:11). In James 3, the reference seems to be to all Christians—not everyone should try to speak up, share, and teach during the assembly. James includes himself in the group of teachers. The reason given for limiting the desire to be teachers is that teachers will be judged more strictly. Teachers are responsible for what they teach.

Teaching is a great responsibility because of how easily we stumble. Everyone stumbles. We are especially prone to stumbling in matters related to our words. In fact, missteps and miscues are so common in our speech that James says someone who gets his talking under control will be able to control every other part of the body. In this context, "perfect" means mature or full-grown. The word seldom communicates the idea of being sinless. James has used this word frequently in the book (1:4, 17, 25; 2:22; 3:2). The person able to control the tongue demonstrates both maturity and self-control.

3:3-5. Horses have been domesticated and can be controlled by putting a small bit in their mouths. A ship is guided by a small rudder, even though the ships themselves are large and the winds that power them are strong. A small spark can cause a huge forest fire. All of these are examples of the power of a small thing, power disproportionate to size. The tongue is in the same category. In proportion to the size of the human body, the tongue is only a small part, but it is pretentious and makes huge boasts. In v. 5, the tongue is personified and can become proud and boastful. The illustrations used in this section show the power of small objects. These illustrations also point to the fact that the tongue is different because it is itself uncontrollable (3:6-8).

3:6-8. What is said in these verses is not difficult to understand. What it means and how it is to be interpreted is more difficult. Considering the nature of wisdom literature, we should expect figures of speech, exaggeration, and poetic language. The greatest barrier the Bible student has to overcome in this passage is the tendency to read the Bible literally.

The tongue is not only like a spark that can begin a fire, the tongue is a fire. This figure of speech, a simile, means the tongue is like a fire. The tongue resembles the world of unrighteousness (*adikia*). Human speech is often unrighteous. Perhaps one could say that human speech is more often unrighteous than righteous. Speech reveals the wickedness of human hearts. Even though it is a small part of the human body, the tongue is a defiling influence. Despite its small size, it can defile the entire body. Its influence in the human body is so great that it sets on fire (*phlogizo*, to inflame, to inflame with passion) the cycle (*trochos*, wheel, circuit, course) of generations (*genesis*, literally birth, by application this word could mean life, nature). The tongue is powerful enough that it impacts the entirety of life (the course of life, the natural cycle) from beginning to end. Throughout one's life, the influence of the tongue can affect future generations. The point of this language is to show the nature of the tongue—fiery, unrighteous, defiling, influential, inflaming.

The last phrase of v. 6 says the tongue is inflamed by "Gehenna." Here is the only New Testament use of this word outside the words of Jesus. The metaphorical meaning is that the unrighteousness of the tongue is itself the result of the influence of evil in one's life. Gehenna refers to the valley south of Jerusalem. The word was used to describe punishment for those who rejected God since it is identified with the place where child sacrifices were offered to Molech in the Old Testament.

Verse 6 may seem a bit mysterious and difficult at first reading. Remember that wisdom literature uses figurative language. The tongue is like a fire, it is like a defiling unrighteousness among the members of the body. Although it is small, it cannot be controlled. It inflames all of one's life for the entirety of one's life. The influence and impact of the tongue never ceases. Where does such evil come from? The tongue reveals the unrighteousness that exists in one's life, as though the tongue itself is inflamed by evil.

3:7. James returns to the illustration of taming animals. Animals can be tamed, even as human beings were given dominion over the creation (Gen. 1:26-28). The animate creation human beings have been able to tame, with the exception of taming themselves.

3:8. This verse summarizes vv. 6-8. No one can tame the tongue, it is a restless (*akatastaton*) evil full of deadly poison.

3:9-12. Verses 1-2 served as an introduction to show the importance of the tongue. Verses 3-5 illustrated the power of small things, thus the power of the tongue. Verses 6-8 showed the uncontrollable evil that the tongue reveals and communicates. The final section (vv. 9-12) speaks to the inconsistency of the tongue in everyday life and experience.

3:9-10. The tongue is used for both blessing God and cursing men. It is not right that blessing and cursing come from the same source; even more, such is unimaginable because the human beings who are being cursed are made in God's likeness. "Lord and Father" may refer to the Son and the Father, or only to the Father. Based on the limited references to Jesus in the book, the second option is preferable. The text is ambiguous, but the validity of the point being made does not depend on which understanding is correct. The point is that blessing is given to deity and curses are pronounced against humanity made in the likeness of God (Gen. 1:26-27). Some think that curses may refer to rivalries among various teachers in the church (3:14).

That both curses and blessings come from the same mouth and same tongue should not occur. "My brothers" in the middle of v. 10 presents an interesting challenge as one tries to apply the theory that the phrase is used to introduce new thoughts or paragraphs. Perhaps it is used here, and in some other places in the book of James, simply to call attention to an important point. The point is this: human speech has a wonderful capacity for good, it can also be used for evil. "These things ought not to be."

3:11-12. Illustrations from nature validate the principle. A fountain cannot give both fresh and bitter water. A fig tree does not produce olives, a (grape) vine does not produce figs. A salt water source cannot produce fresh water. The questions are rhetorical, anticipating negative responses.

3:13-18. The first question of v. 13 connects this section with the preceding. James continues to address the same general topic. "Wise and understanding," understood in the context of the Old Testament, refers to one capable of understanding God's truth and applying it in daily life. The theme of "wisdom" resurfaces. Christians are urged to ask God for wisdom (1:5). One who can use the tongue correctly is wise. We can identify the wise and understanding teacher, not by his words, but by his good manner of life and his gentle (*prautes*, meek, mild, humble) spirit of wisdom. The wise person is not only gentle, he is meek and humble. Good teachers live and teach humbly with a demeanor of meekness. "Let him show" reminds us of 2:18 and 2:20. This wisdom is not evidenced by knowledge that can retrieve mountains of information rapidly. This wisdom is shown by both knowledge and the humility of the heart that gratefully realizes what it means to experience God's goodness and to seek God's guidance to do his will.

3:14-16. Two kinds of wisdom are contrasted in the extended paragraph (3:13-18). There is a "wisdom" that is from below, from the earth. This wisdom, which hardly qualifies to be called wisdom, is described in vv. 14-16. This wisdom is of the world. This wisdom seeks to get ahead and cares little for the needs of others. This wisdom is often reflected by the tongue and its evil. Perhaps a good way to describe it is to say that it is a false wisdom. In the context of Chapter 3, this may be the wisdom of unqualified or unprepared teachers.

Let us not assume too quickly that we easily avoid this danger. Many problems arise when sincere believers (1) overemphasize one truth to the exclusion of other equally important biblical truths, (2) build doctrines and theories on a limited understanding, (3) think they have seen something new that no one else has seen before, (4) validate their teachings with proof-texting, (5) see things through the traditions and teachings they have received without developing a mature wisdom and understanding , and (6) depend on what others have said or written about the Bible, using such writings as their primary resources tools rather than the Word of God. Teachers, and all Christians, who would be wise and understanding must be constantly aware of such fallacies.

One problem that arises with such practices is the tendency to become defensive. A basic cause of defensiveness is egotism. In our defensiveness, we often respond with the attitudes we have learned in the world: bitter (*pikros*) jealousy or envy (*zelos*), selfish ambition (*eritheia*, contention or strife, ambition), and arrogance (especially arrogance that demeans the truth). The phrasing literally reads, "If you have bitter jealousy and contentions in your heart, do not be arrogant and tell lies against the truth." The last two verbs are negative imperatives.

Such wisdom does not descend from above (a metaphorical way to refer to God). This kind of wisdom is worldly, sensual, and demonic. The adjectives can be more easily understood when they are considered with their antonyms: worldly is opposed to heavenly, sensual or natural is opposed to spiritual, demonic is opposed to godly. The result of jealousy and ambition is disorder and all kinds of evil. Bitter jealousy or envy is listed as a sin in Gal. 5:20 and Eph. 4:31.

3:17-18. The last two verses of the chapter describe heavenly wisdom, the wisdom from above. This wisdom is contrasted with the wisdom described in vv. 14-16. First, the wisdom from above is pure (*hagnos*, from the same root as holy). It is undefiled. It is peaceful (*eirenikos*, see Heb. 12:11 for another use of the same word), gentle (*epieikes*, moderate, patient), and accommodating (*eupeithes*, compliant, easily entreated, reasonable). Here is the only occurrence of the word *eupeithes* in the New Testament. Continuing, this wisdom is full of mercy (*eleos*) and good fruits. The two concepts combine attitude and action. The meaning is "full of mercy and also full of good fruits." This wisdom is impartial (*adiakritos*, not judgmental or prejudiced) and without hypocrisy (*anupokritos*, sincere, transparent).

James concludes with what sounds like a proverb. This may serve as a conclusion to vv. 17-18; it could also serve as a fitting conclusion to vv. 13-18. Loosely, "peacemakers who sow peace reap righteousness." Similar phrasing occurs in Prov. 11:30; Isa. 32:16-17; Amos 6:12; 2 Cor. 9:10; Gal. 5:22; Phil. 1:11; Heb. 12:11. The fruit of righteousness is sown in peace by those who make peace. The fruit of righteousness is fruit that consists of righteousness. Righteousness is the result when peacemakers peacefully sow and cultivate the fruit of righteousness. Peace is a central aspect of wisdom.

The righteousness of v. 18 contrasts with the evil practices of v. 16. Note that there is a right way to sow righteousness and a wrong way. Righteousness is the result of peacemakers, not contentious persons. Wisdom from above seeks harmony. Worldly wisdom is characterized by envy, selfishness, ambition, contention, disrupted relationships. The characteristics of heavenly wisdom are exactly the opposites of the characteristics of worldly wisdom.

Final Reflections on the Chapter

Before we leave Chapter 3, it is worth noting again that the original text did not contain the chapter divisions we have today. The chapter and verse divisions were added later. As we transition to Chapter 4, a major point in reading and understanding the text is to try to identify the nature of the transition. Are there points of connection between the two chapters, or does James begin a new thought in 4:1?

James 4

[Note: it is suggested that the student read the introductory materials in this guide before beginning any individual preparatory reading and analysis.]

CONTENT
The outline and paragraphing included in the Content section of each chapter are only suggestions or guides. The student is encouraged to identify the paragraphs and subsections within each paragraph to assist in his or her own study. In this chapter, the division of the biblical text into paragraphs is fairly standard in modern translations.

Outline of the Chapter
4:1-6	Contrast between worldliness and godliness
4:7-10	The cure for worldliness
4:11-12	Godliness avoids judging one another
4:13-17	Warning against self-confidence

    Note: this warning continues into Chapter 5.

Overview of the Chapter
    The chapter begins with two rhetorical questions, reflecting James's use of diatribe, a literary technique that uses a supposed objector to provide a contrast to the message presented by the author. This technique is common in James (2:14-26; 3:13).

    The first section continues the contrast between worldliness and godliness. The question — whether the "you" (vv. 1-3) refers specifically to the recipients, or is used in a more generic sense of the objector who represents worldliness — is important for understanding and interpretation (see Study Helps for more on this point). The influence of worldliness, the temptation of worldly wisdom, is a constant struggle in the life of the Christian and in the church. The specific application may relate to rivalries between church leaders (3:1).

    To hear Christians referred to as adulteresses, sinners, and double-minded (1:6-8) should catch our attention. Because of the attractiveness of the world and the influence of the devil, the Christian life is not easy. If vv. 1-6 present the problem and show that worldliness is the cause of conflict, desires, and quarrels, vv. 7-10 present the solution. These verses should be read in relation to the use of the tongue and the two types of wisdom described in Chapter 3.

In vv. 7-10, ten imperatives give instructions for life. This short, choppy, disconnected structure is characteristic of wisdom literature.

Verses 11-12 seem to summarize and close the section about the tongue. The topic of human speech was first mentioned in 1:19. These two verses also reflect 2:12-13 where judgment was forbidden.

Some have seen in 4:17 a closing summary while others see the topic of misplaced confidence extending into 5:1-6. The desire to identify transition points and outlines show how difficult it is to read the book as wisdom literature and moral instruction. Such outlining would seldom be attempted in the book of Proverbs where certain themes surface again and again. Perhaps we should also avoid the temptation to outline too strictly in the book of James.

STUDY HELPS

4:1-6. Two rhetorical questions focus the matter the author will address. Quarrels, conflicts, and pleasures are concepts that appeared in Chapter 3. Why do these exist in the lives of Christians? Why do these exist in the church? These questions do not introduce new topics. They provide a transition to an expanded explanation and treatment of the problem being addressed. The subject of 4:1-6 is the contrast between worldliness and godliness. The problems in the church are not from God. They are not the product of the wisdom from above.

Consider this brief summary of Chapter 4. Worldliness in the church causes quarrels, conflicts, wars, lusts, murder, envy, and fights. Personal attacks replace harmony and peace (3:18). Prayer is misfocused, judging is common, Christians arrogantly try to direct their own lives.

4:1-3. Quarrels (*polemos*, fighting, battles) and conflicts (*mache*, striving, controversy, contention) are the result of sensual delights (*hedone*, desires, lusts, pleasures; the Greek word is the root of our word hedonism). The word *hedone* refers to putting one's own desires first. These desires make war (*strateuomai*, contend, as in warfare) within us. This verb is the root of our word strategy. Problems with others come from the problems inside us. Desires are pictured as fighting inside us, strategically maneuvering to gain advantage. In this passage, the specific reference is to the members of the body (cf. 3:6), then by extension to members of the church.

4:2-3. Despite problems with punctuation and phrasing, one should see the parallelism in vv. 1-3. The meaning of the text is not in doubt—only how to divide (or connect) the words. Verse 2 repeats words and ideas from v. 1. Desires are unfulfilled (you do not have), which results in violence when efforts are made to obtain what is desired. Personal efforts to obtain take the place of asking God. The verbs in the passage are these: *epithumeo* (to desire or covet), *phoneuo* (to kill or murder), *zeloo* (to envy or be jealous), *epitugchano* (to obtain), *machomai* (to fight), and *polemeo* (to fight).

Some translations have "to envy" instead of "to kill," based on an unsubstantiated manuscript change by Erasmus, a change that was later followed by others and by some translations. The manuscript evidence supports "to murder," perhaps in the sense of intense hatred (cf. Matt. 5:21-26, also to be classified as wisdom literature). Wisdom literature often uses exaggerated statements to make a point. One must address the question of whether some of the recipients were murderers, or if the description is perhaps a generic way of describing worldliness. Another option is that the recipients would have experienced such things in their former, pre-Christian life, but this option seems less likely considering that the majority of the recipients were Jewish Christians and that their former lives would have been lived according to strict Old Testament teachings.

Christians struggle due to improper motives and lack of prayer. Lack of prayer is the result of lack of trust in God. James describes some whose motives in prayer were to receive more things that could be used selfishly to fulfill personal desires. Prayer is not a way for the Christian to obtain what she or he wants. Prayer is about God's will, not our will. For the Christian, lack of prayer must be remedied. Misguided and misfocused prayer must be recognized and corrected.

4:4. "Adulteresses," a feminine form, refers to spiritual adultery not physical. One cannot be a friend of God and a friend of the world at the same time. Remember that this verse follows a paragraph that contrasts God's wisdom and worldly wisdom. One cannot have both. A choice must be made.

4:5-6. In these two verses we come to a difficult text. First, there is a textual variant between the intransitive verb "the spirit that lives in us" and the causative verb "the spirit that he causes to live in us." The latter form is better attested in the manuscript evidence and is to be preferred. In addition, the specific scriptural text to which v. 5 refers is not certain, so we receive no help by reading the cited passage in its original context. Third, is there one question or two? (The ASV illustrates the use of two questions: Or think ye that the scripture speaketh in vain? Doth the spirit which he made to dwell in us long unto envying?) Finally, depending on how one answers the previous questions, the application of the verb construction "to yearn enviously" will vary.

So that the reader will fully understand the nature of the difficulties, here is the text rendered literally: "do you think that in vain the scripture says for envy longs the spirit which he causes to dwell in us." The Greek text does not have a capital "S" or small "s" to guide the interpretation of the verse. The two options are these. First, he (God) enviously (jealously) desires the Spirit that he made to dwell in us. Second, the spirit that he made to dwell in us enviously (jealously) desires (longs).

Before treating the question of interpretation, we should note that v. 6 is part of the extended context: "He gives greater grace, therefore it says, 'God opposes the proud but gives grace to the humble.'" This quotation, the second in the context, is from Prov. 3:34 (LXX). The two verses (vv. 5-6) should be understood as a unit.

The first option mentioned above says that God longs for his Spirit that dwells in us. The thought seems incomplete without something additional, for example, God longs for his Spirit to guide us. God does not desire hostility but relationship. He makes relationship continually possible through his indwelling Spirit so that Christians do not seek friendship with the world. Against this interpretation is the fact that James has not previously mentioned the Holy Spirit. If this verse is understood to refer to the Holy Spirit, this verse will be the only reference to the Holy Spirit in the book of James. In the early years of Christianity, we have no evidence of a well-developed theology of the Holy Spirit. These observations are sufficient cause to question the first option, even though they are not conclusive.

The second option says that the spirit that God makes to dwell in human beings (the human spirit) enviously desires. Contextually, the meaning would be something like this: the desires that are mentioned in vv. 1-4 are the result of the natural envious longing of the (human) spirit that God made to dwell in us.

4:6. "God gives greater grace." In my opinion, the context holds together best by using the second option. God gives grace that is greater than mankind's sin problems. The human spirit naturally longs with envy, but God gives grace. God opposes the proud and gives grace to the humble, recalling the contrast of the two kinds of wisdom in 3:13-18.

4:7-10. These verses contain 10 imperatives. This kind of construction is common in wisdom literature. While the imperatives are not totally random and disconnected, neither is it easy to find a sequential pattern or to identify the connections. The imperatives are fairly simple and appear with little amplification.

4:7. Submit to God. Because of the transitional particle, so or then (*oun*), it seems that what is said in 4:7 and verses following is connected to what has already been said.

4:7. Resist the devil, and he will flee from you. Resist means to stands against. It is often noted that there are two opposing tensions in the Christian life: submitting to the good and resisting the evil.

4:8. Draw near to God. Although God has drawn near to humanity in Jesus, this verse says that God will continue to draw near to us because we are drawing near to him. God faithfully responds to our faith.

4:8. Cleanse your hands, you sinners. All have sinned, and Christians are sinners in need of continuous cleansing by the blood of Christ (1 John 1:8-10). That Christians are addressed as sinners catches one's attention. Sinners need cleansing. Cleansing the hands was important in Judaism and carried over into the first century in a number of traditions. The phrase as used here likely means "cleanse your lives." Clean hands sometimes referred to a pure life (see 1 Tim. 2:8, lifting holy hands in prayer).

4:8. Purify your hearts, you double-minded (cf. 1:8). The general meaning of this command is similar to the previous one. Both hands and heart are to be pure. These two commands, taken together, may suggest the need for outward cleansing in a pure life, and inward cleansing of the heart. One must have a singular focus on the things of God to succeed in the Christian life. There is no place for dual allegiances or loyalties.

4:9. Be miserable, mourn, weep. I have grouped these three imperatives. They are either parallel or sequential. To overcome sin (the subject of 4:8), one must find sin repulsive and mourn and weep spiritually. These verbs may refer to repentance.

4:9. Let your laughter be turned to mourning. Christianity is not all joy. Sorrow often precedes joy.

4:10. Humble yourselves. Humility is a Christian necessity. Especially in a time of conflicts and quarrels, the humble spirit of peace is essential (3:17-18). One who humbles self will be exalted by God.

4:11-12. "Brothers" may introduce a new discourse section. Note the use of "brothers" in v. 11 to refer to two groups—the ones who are criticizing and the ones being criticized. Do not speak against (*katalaleo*, present imperative, often indicates continuing action, thus an act currently in progress, with the negative imperative meaning to stop) one another (cf. 5:9). Talking against and judging (*krino*) a brother is equal to talking against the law and judging the law. A judgmental attitude contradicts the law, in essence saying that the law is not valid or valuable. The "law" mentioned is likely the "law of love" that was previously mentioned in 2:8, 12 where it was identified with the "law of liberty" of 1:25. It is not possible to be a doer of the law (1:22, be doers and not merely hearers) while one is a judge. "Of the law" does not appear at the end of v. 11 in the original text.

4:12. Further, how can you be a judge, seeing that "One is Lawgiver and Judge, the One who is able to save and destroy"? "One" in the primary position is emphatic. The verse should not be understood as teaching Jewish monotheism in opposition to Christian trinitarianism. The usage reflects Old Testament terminology that was well-known among Jewish Christians in the early decades of Christianity. There is no place for Christians to judge their neighbors. Such reflects worldly wisdom and the misuse of the tongue. Criticizing others to make oneself appear better should not be part of the fellowship of believers.

4:13-17. Who are the ones being addressed in these verses? Is this another diatribe against a supposed objector? Is James referring to a specific group? While the answers to such questions are conjecture, the point of the paragraph is not. Here is an admonition against arrogant and misplaced self-confidence. Those who do not take God into account in their planning fail to acknowledge God's will in the events of the world. This is another example of worldly wisdom that thinks primarily of self.

Life is as a mist (*atmis*, compare our word atmosphere). The frailty of human life is a common wisdom theme. The Greek words for appear (*phaino*) and vanish (*aphanizo*, disappear) sound similiar.

4:15-16. The third class condition communicates contingent action. Whatever happens in our life is dependent on the will of God. "If the Lord will" is a good reminder of God's presence in our lives. James urges his readers to be aware of God's will in their lives in a healthy way spiritually. Some Christians today so pepper their speech with this phrase that the idea becomes meaningless. Often the phrase is used as an excuse or as an explanation. Let us never forget the importance of understanding biblical teaching in context. These verses are not an explanation of evil, natural disasters, random violence: "if God will." Such is a misapplication of this text. These verses address the boastful, arrogant attitude that excludes God from daily life six days a week and salutes him only on Sunday. Such boasting is evil. In the book of James, there is a proper source of glorying

(1:9-10) and there are improper motivations for self-glorying, as in 4:15-16.

4:17. The connection of this statement to the surrounding context may not be apparent, but the careful student will take time to explore the possibilities. Consider first that the transitional particle "then" or "therefore" bases v. 17 on what has come before. Is the focus on knowing the right thing to do, or is the focus on failure to act? Many Christians define sin with a list of things to be avoided. Sin is what one does. In this verse, sin is what one does not do. Sin is failure to act. In our study of the book of James to this point, a long list of examples could be developed to illustrate this truth. Here is what you should do and failing to do it is sin! In addition, the analysis of the verse should not only look backward ("therefore"), it should also look forward to Chapter 5. (Remember that the chapter divisions were added later and may artificially divide the biblical text in some cases.)

James 5

[Note: it is suggested that the student read the introductory materials in this guide before beginning individual preparatory reading and analysis.]

CONTENT

The outline and paragraphing included in the Content section of each chapter are only suggestions or guides. The student is encouraged to identify the paragraphs and subsections within each paragraph to assist in his or her own study. The division of the biblical text into paragraphs is fairly standard in modern translations.

<u>Outline of the Chapter</u>
5:1-6	Warning to the rich and self-confident
5:7-12	Patience and perseverance in prayer, anticipating the Lord's coming
5:13-18	The prayer of faith is powerful in meeting needs
5:19-20	Bringing back those who have wandered

<u>Overview of the Chapter</u>

The first verses of this chapter (5:1-6) are part of an extended paragraph that contains warnings against self-confidence and depending on riches (beginning in 4:13). James frequently mentions the rich and the poor. A good way to frame the matter James raises is this: what is an appropriate attitude toward wealth for the Christian? The problem with wealth is that human desires and possessions tend to focus our attention on the things of this world rather than on God.

While the return of Jesus is not a primary theme in James, neither is it absent. James assumes the immediate return of the Lord. In anticipation of Jesus' return, James urges patience on the part of the believers. Examples of patience in the second section (5:7-12) include the farmer, the prophets, and Job. James' emphasis on the proper use of the tongue also continues (5:9, 12).

A primary theme in the final section of the book (5:13-20) is the importance and place of prayer. The church that is committed to prayer will find power to overcome a host of problems and meet a number of needs. In prayer, the church effectively addresses suffering, illness, sin, and unfaithfulness.

STUDY HELPS

5:1-6. "Come now" is parallel to 4:13. The phrase is often identified with diatribe. Diatribe uses a supposed opponent to present a truth. In 5:1-6, a truth is set forth and possible reactions are then presented. The paragraph is reminiscent of Old Testament wisdom literature, the Old Testament prophets, and Jesus' teachings, especially in the Sermon on the Mount.

5:1. The rich are either rich believers (1:10) or rich unbelievers (2:1-7). The integration of the rich and the poor in the first century church was often a problem (1 Cor. 11:17ff). There were rich persons in the early church (see for example, Rom. 16:1; 1 Tim. 6:9-10, 17). The verbs (weep, howl) seem to point to coming judgment. In 4:9, weeping was connected with coming near to God. Here, it is associated with judgment. In 5:1, there is an imperative followed by a participle. In this kind of construction, the participle has an imperatival sense (see Matt. 28:19 for a well-known example). The approaching miseries (*talaiporia*, wretchedness, calamity) can be anticipated. In Judaism, wealth was understood as a blessing from God but it carried with it covenant responsibilities. Judgment was promised to those who misused their wealth.

5:2-3. Clothing and metals were signs of wealth. The riches (*ploutos*) are corrupted (*sepo*, putrefy) and the clothing is moth-eaten. The metals, gold and silver, are rusted (*katioo*, corrode). These descriptions show that the wealth was excessive, and that it was being stored instead of being used. The ruined excess will be a witness against the rich. These teachings remind one of Jesus and the Sermon on the Mount (Matt. 6:19-20). Riches figuratively "eat a person up." Human beings are easily consumed with wealth, "as fire."

"You have hoarded treasure in the last days." The point is this. With the appearing of the last days, everyone should recognize that it is time to seek deliverance and to avoid condemnation. Instead of using God's blessings to be prepared for the sure judgment that is associated with the last days, the rich have increased the certainty of God's judgment upon them. How absurd is it to store up excess in the last days!

"Last days" is an Old Testament concept that was associated with both times of blessing and times of judgment. In the Old Testament, the Messiah would come in the last days in order to bless God's people, but the last days would also be a time of judgment against both God's people and the nations. In the Old Testament, the "last days" referred at times to the end of the Jewish nation. In the New Testament, "last days" is again used at times to refer to the end of the Jewish nation. Given that Christians also suffered when Judaism was destroyed (Matthew 24), the reference in James 5 may be to the end of Judaism. "Last days" also refers in the New Testament to Jesus' coming in judgment, most commonly associated with his coming or return. The interpretation that "last days" in these verses anticipates the coming judgment of Jesus' return is the most widely accepted view.

5:4-6. The rich landowners hired laborers from among the poor and then failed to pay wages. In the first century, day laborers needed their pay every day to provide the basic necessities of life. The rich often delayed payment to ensure that the workers would return the following day. The textual variant (one reading says "to withhold wages" while another says "to deprive or to defraud") makes little difference in the meaning of the verse. Abuse of the poor cries out (*krazo*, this strong verb can be translated shriek) against the rich. The cries (*boe*) of the reapers are heard by God, the Lord of hosts (literally, Lord of Sabaoth). Sabaoth (a transliteration of the Hebrew word, *tsebha'oth*) is not to be confused with Sabbath. These are two different and unrelated words.

Against the rich, James levels the accusation: you have indulged in luxury and have lived in pleasure, you have pampered your hearts (*trepho*, to pamper with food, to fatten) as in preparation for slaughter. The meaning is parallel to v. 3, anticipating the return of the Lord and judgment. The condemnation of the righteous was most likely the result of exploiting the poor and outcasts, or of failure to take care of them. In the reference to killing the righteous (*phoneuo*, to murder, same word as was used in 4:2), the question raised in the discussion of 4:2 comes up again. Are these references to Christians or to unbelievers? Is the reference to murder to be understood as an example of exaggeration, meaning violence and hatred? Or is the reference to actions before these became Christians? The latter possibility seems less likely given the context. James seems to be addressing present realities (although the verbs are aorist past tense). In the mistreatment of the righteous, the disempowered and weak in the society can offer no resistance.

5:7-12. "Brothers" may serve to introduce a new paragraph or section, but "therefore" (*oun*) connects v. 7 to the previous verses. Because of the realities set forth in 5:1-6, believers are admonished to be patient (*makrothumeo*, long-suffering, aorist imperative) until the coming (*parousia*) of the Lord. *Parousia* is the usual word to describe Jesus' return. The theme of patience appears four times in this brief section (twice in v. 7, v. 8, v. 10). The farmer is the first of three examples of patience. Christians are urged to be patient and strengthen (*sterizo*) their hearts because the coming (*parousia*) is near.

5:9. In the midst of the teachings concerning patience is another reference to speech and judging. The use of "brothers" so quickly after v. 7 must be for the purpose of catching attention or emphasizing an important point. In the midst of life's challenges, do not grumble (*stenazo*) against one another, because such grumbling leads to judgment. Given the immediacy of judgment, one hardly desires to expose oneself to greater judgment. This verse clearly connects with 2:12-13 and 4:11-12.

5:10-11. The use of "brothers" in v. 10 is noteworthy, if only for the repetition of the word in this section. Two more examples of patience are the Old Testament prophets and Job. The prophets are among those who experienced suffering (*kakopatheia*) and exhibited endurance (*makrothumia*); they endured (*hupomeno*).

Job was known proverbially for his endurance. Some translations have patience instead of endurance. Endurance is preferred. Some students of the book of Job have noted that Job, rather than being an example of patience, was really quite impatient! To say Job endured is accurate; to say Job endured patiently less so. The point of the examples, especially of the prophets and of Job, is to observe the way the compassionate merciful Lord deals with his people to work out his will. The Lord is compassionate (*polusplagchnos*) and merciful (*oiktirmon*). The adjectives used are unusual and rare in the New Testament.

5:12. "My brothers" should be noted. "Above all" is a way of concluding. This phrase serves less as an indicator of a new subject and more as a way to introduce a brief summary of the extended section about the use of the tongue, a section that began in 3:1. Misuse of the tongue subjects one to judgment. The tongue must be carefully guarded, even in times of mistreatment and suffering. Our words are important.

5:13-18. In the face of abuse by the rich, the proper response is patient perseverance as one anticipates the Lord's coming. The prophets and Job suffered long. The word James uses for patience means long-suffering. Now another response is introduced. Prayers of faith are powerful in meeting needs. Prayer is an appropriate response to suffering. Praise is an appropriate response to blessings. Corporate prayer is an appropriate response to weakness.

This paragraph raises several difficult questions. What is the nature of the infirmity (literally, weakness)? Is it physical, spiritual, or does the text have a double application? In the early church, what was the role of the church in physical healing? Why were some Christians healed physically while others were not? What was the role of various actions or symbols in the healing process?

One way to summarize these verses is to note that they deal with the proper use of the tongue. Another is to say that these verses deal with the importance and power of prayer. Christians are people of prayer, praying for themselves individually and praying for one another.

5:13-14. These verses have three imperatives, all of which are third person singular imperatives, "Let him...." The last imperative has received the most attention in studies of James because it is the most difficult to understand. "If anyone among you is weak *(astheneo*, without strength), let him call for the elders of the church." The Greek word is used in the New Testament to refer to both physical weakness and spiritual weakness. The ambiguity may be purposeful, but it is also perplexing. In the first century, sin and sickness were often associated (John 9:2). Is the weakness of 5:14 to be associated with the suffering of 5:13? The reason for calling the elders is so they can pray over the person, anointing him with oil in the name of the Lord. The plural noun suggests that all of the elders in the local assembly were involved, although the grammar requires only a plurality. The most likely context is the home of the weak or sick person, referring to a private meeting. These verses would not refer to the assembly, since the instructions suggest calling the elders to a place they would not otherwise be. The elders are identified as the elders of the church (assembly).

Let them (the elders) pray over him (the verb is another third person imperative). Prayer is frequently mentioned in this section: let him pray (v. 13), let them pray (v. 14), the prayer of faith (v. 15), pray for one another (v. 16), effective prayer (v. 16), Elijah prayed (v. 17), he prayed again (v. 18). Anointing is a participle that depends on the verb, "let them pray." To arrive at an accurate understanding of this passage demands that we spend a little time with the word that is translated anointing.

What was the nature of the anointing? The word *aleipho* (anoint) used here is not the common word for religious anointing (*chrio*, the noun is *chrisma*, compare our word christen). *Aleipho* was commonly used for applying medicine by rubbing. Another Greek verb (*murizo*) was used to describe anointing for burial (Mk. 14:8). *Aleipho*, the word in 5:14, was also used for anointing for burial (Mk. 16:1), anointing the sick (Mk. 6:13), and anointing oneself in Judaism (Matt. 6:17). It is used in Luke 7 when a sinful woman anoints Jesus. *Chrio* is used in the New Testament with a spiritual significance. Two related verbs, *egchrio* and *epichrio*, are used in Rev. 3:18 for rubbing on salve.

Oil was used in the first century medicinally, symbolically, and ceremonially to prepare for being in God's presence. Oil was used in daily life prior to daily activities, especially on joyful occasions. "In the name of the Lord" means by the power or authority of the Lord. To associate this phrase only with the anointing and not with the praying is not supported by the grammar of the text. The word order indicates that the phrase applies to both. These verses (5:13-14) do not seem to be related to the gift of healing mentioned in 1 Cor. 12. The group involved here is the elders of the local assembly.

Based on these factors, it seems that the primary application of this passage in the first century was to physical ailments or weaknesses, especially those that caused physical suffering. The elders were called primarily to pray in the name of the Lord and the anointing with oil was done medicinally (for relief from suffering?).

5:15. In the context, the prayer (*euche*) of faith applies most immediately to the prayer of the elders although the phrase could extend backward to the prayer of 5:13, in times of suffering. The prayer of faith, offered by the elders, will save (*sozo*) the sick one (*kamno*, wearied, faint, sickened). Note the change of terminology referring to the sick one—from weakness (*astheneo*) to wearied (*kamno*).

The normal understanding is that the word "to save" relates to spiritual salvation, but the word is also used of physical deliverance (Matt. 9:22, Mk. 6:56). The first part of the context relates to physical healing. The person wearied and faint will be raised up by the Lord in response to the prayer of faith. The second part of the verse addresses a second matter. If the wearied person has committed sins, the prayer of faith is effective also for forgiving sins. The verse clearly separates the physical weakness from the possibility of sin having been committed.

The context of 5:13-15 relates to believers with physical problems of weakness, perhaps involving suffering (v. 13). Elders of the church pray in faith, in the name of the Lord. They rub the person with oil medicinally, and the person is made b0etter by the Lord. The prayer of the elders can also work toward the forgiveness of any sins that the weakened person has committed. The historical context of the first century is a time period in which medical doctors were not readily available as they are today. The historical context of the text is somewhat parallel to the pioneering spirit of my grandmother 100 ycars ago, when most physical ailments were treated with salve, poultices, liniment, and other "home remedies."

Should 5:13-15 be considered an example for the church today? Do the verses rise to the level of a mandate so that elders should be seeking such opportunities? First, note that the text places the first responsibility on the person who is weak, "let him call for the elders." Certainly, today there exist problems which the medics cannot solve. Suffering, weakness, and fatigue may have spiritual roots. The prayers of faith offered by mature Christians are desirable in such circumstances. However, with medical treatments more readily available today, one can also see where the application of these verses would be less frequent.

5:16. Of great importance to understanding this verse is the connection to what has gone before, "therefore" (*oun*). Based on what has just been said, "you (plural) confess to one another sins and you (plural) pray for one another so that you (plural) may be healed (*iaomai*, made whole)." The confession of sins is an imperative command, but in what context is this to be done? Is this a new subject so that James has now moved from the subject of prayer for physical needs to the subject of prayer for spiritual needs, including the confession of sins? Has James moved from the subject of elders praying to the topic of every Christian praying? Or is this a continuation of the previous context related to elders praying for both physical needs and spiritual needs. Does v. 16 tell how the prayer of faith of the elders is to be accomplished? Why is there a change of verb from *sozo* to *iaomai*?

An important matter is whether the application of "to save" (*sozo*) means physical deliverance (as in 5:15) or spiritual deliverance. Considering the context, one must also read ahead to 5:19-20 where the same verb (*sozo*) is used in a spiritual sense. The question is not easy to resolve. The move from "elders" to "one another" and the use of the word *sozo* in 5:20 suggest a spiritual application. The overall context of healing that comes through confession and prayer, with the example of Elijah, suggests the continuation of physical applications.

"Confess your sins" is a plural imperative, meaning it applies to all of the readers. Confession is an important part of healing. Confession is a corrective against self-confidence, mistreatment of others, inappropriate speech, and selfish attitudes.

Confession is a corrective against the wisdom of the world. Confession is cleansing for the person confessing.

"To one another" could mean to other Christians as appropriate, including to the elders, with specific application to vv. 13-15. Biblically, confession is also to be made to those wronged. Some sin in the early church had to be handled publicly, perhaps because knowledge of the sin was public. Sin would be confessed to the elders, since the elders could hardly pray about a sin if they did not know about it. Sin is first confessed to God and then to the church leaders. Sin is confessed to those wronged. Is sin also to be confessed publicly to the entire church? Many interpret this passage today to say that "to one another" does not literally mean "to one another," but instead means to a select group of closest friends or confidants.

"Pray for one another" is another plural imperative. All (you, plural) are to pray so that all (you, plural) will be healed. As *sozo* can be applied to both physical and spiritual deliverance, so also *iaomai* has the same breadth of meaning. The change of Greek words may be nothing more than the use of synonyms for literary interest.

Literally, "The prayer (*deesis*) of a righteous person is very powerful in its working." This seems to apply the responsibility of prayer more broadly than only to the elders. Upright and persistent persons pray effectively. Note the change in the word for prayer. To understand this verse in context, remember that we are reading wisdom literature and that the teachings are generalizations. Here is the general principle: when righteous people pray, God works powerfully in response.

In summary, because prayer is an effective antidote to suffering and weakness, one should pray. When faced with such circumstances, one should ask mature Christian leaders (elders) to pray. Their prayer of faith can restore physical strength and bring forgiveness of sins. In such circumstances, all Christians should involve the church (one another) in prayer in order to find wholeness of body and spirit. The proper response to suffering, weakness, and sin is always patient perseverance in prayer.

5:17-18. Elijah shared our human nature. He was no better and no stronger than are we. When he prayed, it did not rain for three and a half years. When he prayed again, rain fell. Elijah is an example of patient, persevering prayer.

5:19-20. "My brothers" introduces the final paragraph. These two verses may relate directly to 5:13-18, but I have chosen to treat them separately. This illustrates again the problem of wisdom literature with its constant jumping from one topic to another, often stringing together related topics. The instruction is for all of the readers. The church has a role in reclaiming the wanderer; every Christian has a role in reclaiming those who stray.

The third class condition is used to indicate contingency. Two conditions can be noted in the statement: if a believer strays, if another believer is willing to bring the wanderer back. To stray (*planao*, to wander, the root of our word planet) may have doctrinal applications, but in the context, it appears the point is primarily moral, related to sin and weakness. The verb may be passive voice or it may function as a reflexive, causes oneself to wander. In the passive voice it means that outside influences are involved in the wandering. The verb voice is interesting but does not change the meaning of the passage. All Christians have a responsibility to all other Christians. When someone wanders, and someone turns him back (*epistrepho*), the result is this: the one who turns a sinner from the wandering (*plane*) of his way will save (*sozo*) his soul from death and cover a large number of sins.

The idea of wandering, the description of a sinner, and the salvation of the soul from death seem to make the verb *sozo* (save) apply to spiritual death. The modern church struggles to read this passage in context. First, we are not very serious about restoring the fallen and the wanderers. Second, we are not very quick to admit that sin causes death—at times sin causes physical death, without repentance and restoration it causes spiritual death, and eventually it causes eternal death.

To cover a number of sins suggests that the saving relates to sin. Sinners can be reclaimed. Salvation can be lost; salvation becomes a reality for those reclaimed.

A Final Word

If one reads James as a letter, one is likely to be disappointed by the ending. There is no typical closing, no personal greetings, no blessing of grace and peace. We read the book, and then it ends abruptly. We get no summary, no connecting the dots of the various themes that have been presented.

I hope that the absence of a closing is sufficient to cause you to go back and review the letter one more time. Avoid the tendency to read literally. Read between the lines, recognize the generalizations.

Even more, I pray that you will find in the book of James new insights and new motivation. I hope you will find and be able to succeed in a new commitment to controlling your speech, a new commitment to the wisdom from above, a new commitment to demonstrating faith with your actions, and a new commitment to others—meeting physical needs and turning souls to God eternally. One who turns a soul to God saves a soul from eternal death.

Introduction to First Peter

I first did an in-depth study of the letters written by Peter when I was an undergraduate student at Oklahoma Christian College. During the summer trimester of 1969, I enrolled in a class taught by Dr. Raymond Kelcy. Coincidentally, he was at the same time working on a commentary in the series published by the R. B. Sweet Company. He had agreed to write a commentary over the Letters of Peter and Jude. When the commentary was published in 1972 and I purchased a copy, I saw that the notes I took in class were very much like the contents of the commentary.

I recall that he encouraged those of us in the class to work on special projects and studies of various passages, insisting that we provide good academic documentation. Later, I thought that we were likely assisting him in the research for the commentary. When we came to the end of the term, my grade was hovering on the borderline between a high "B" and a low "A." I asked Dr. Kelcy if I could do another paper to help improve my grade. In the next class period, he announced to the entire class that another paper, not required but optional, could be submitted to add points to the final grade. He specifically asked me to research 1 Peter 5:12-14. Even today, when I occasionally refer to his commentary, I fondly remember a summer in the General Letters, and especially the studies in 1 Peter, 2 Peter, and Jude. My notes from the class have long ago been lost, but I still hear echoes of my beloved professor when I consult his commentary. The reader should not be surprised if my observations in this Bible Study Guide at times reflect the positions taken by one of my favorite Bible professors.

<u>Authorship</u>

The author of 1 Peter identifies himself as the apostle Peter (1:1). Strong evidence, both internal and external, supports that view. In addition to the specific statement of 1:1, the author was an eyewitness of Jesus' words and experiences (5:1). His instruction to the elders (5:2) is much like the words Jesus spoke to Peter (John 21:15-17). Similarities between Peter's sermons in Acts and various passages in 1 Peter have been noted. Some have questioned whether Peter could write high quality Greek, but the objection is not based in biblical teaching. Acts 4:13 may mean only that Peter was "unlettered," that is, that he had not received training in a recognized rabbinical school. Palestine was bilingual and Peter had heard Greek spoken all his life. If Silas served as a scribe or secretary (in biblical studies, often referred to as an amanuensis), some of the Greek style may be the result of the writing process.

External evidence is strong and early. Irenaeus (AD 185) quotes the book and attributes the citation to Peter. Tertullian (c. AD 200) and Clement of Alexandria (c. AD 200) likewise credit Peter with the book. The book was accepted early by the church. Clement of Rome in his *Letter to the Corinthians* (AD 93-95) has statements that parallel statements in 1 Peter. That others were familiar with the book is seen in the writings of Papias (AD 130-140), Polycarp (d. AD 155), and Justin Martyr (d. AD 163-165). Among those who question Peter's authorship, the fact that the book is not included in the Muratorian Fragment, a list of canonical books from AD 185-200 is often cited. However, it must also be noted that the Muratorian Fragment is damaged and missing at least one line of text (Westcott, *A General Survey of the History of the Canon of the New Testament*). Based on internal and external evidence, there is no reason not to accept Peter's authorship.

Acceptance into the New Testament Canon

The book is listed in Eusebius' *Ecclesiastical History* as one of the "undisputed books." The early church accepted the book as written by Peter. The question of the canonicity of Peter's letters was made more difficult by the large number of pseudepigraphal writings that bore Peter's name. Pseudepigraphal writings are those writings that had the name of a well-known author attached to give the writing more weight or authority.

Date and Place of Writing

The date is related to authorship, so that those denying Peter's authorship will also attribute a later date to the book. The traditional date is around AD 60. If Peter and Paul were both victims of Nero's reign of terror, as tradition holds, they were likely martyred around AD 65. The date for 1 Peter should be placed in the early 60s.

Peter refers to "she who is at Babylon" (5:13). It is generally thought that Peter was in "Babylon" when he wrote. The question is, which Babylon? Babylon on the Euphrates is a possibility, but that Peter is referring figuratively to a church as "she" and to the city of Rome as "Babylon" is more likely. There is no evidence that Peter was ever in Babylon on the Euphrates, and even stranger would be the possibility that he, Mark, and Silas were all there at the same time. Some of the Patristic writers mentioned above report that the book was written in Rome.

Recipients

The letter is addressed to "the elect exiles of the dispersion," residing in Roman provinces located in northern Asia Minor, what is now northern Turkey. "Chosen" and "exiles of the dispersion" were often used to refer to Jews but are likely used by Peter to refer to the church, God's new Israel. (See James 1:1 for a similar case, referring to Jewish Christians in the early church as "the twelve tribes.")

How the gospel had arrived in these regions is not clear. Paul may have established some churches in these areas (Acts 16). Aquila and Priscilla were from Pontus. Perhaps some Jewish converts had returned home after Pentecost (Acts 2:9-11). The churches were probably begun by Jewish believers but included Gentiles by the 60s. Several phrases in the book suggest a Gentile element among the recipients (e.g. 1:14 and 4:3). Peter also cites the Old Testament several times, suggesting that his readers were aware of Old Testament Scriptures.

Purpose of the Book

Many New Testament letters have both a doctrinal and a practical emphasis. In Paul's letters, the first part is often doctrinal and the second practical. Peter does not maintain such a clear separation, often merging explanation and exhortation. The book is not easy to outline. Given the focus on suffering and persecution, it appears the purpose of the book was to encourage Christians who were experiencing such problems to continue faithfully. Jesus' sufferings (1:11; 2:21, 23; 3:18; 4:1, 13; 5:1) provide an example to follow (1:6-7; 2:19; 3:13-17; 4:1, 12-19; 5:9-10).

Genre of the Book

The book has the typical elements of the Greek letter form, both in the opening salutation and the closing. The opening verses mention the author and the recipients, and include a prayer. The closing greetings include a blessing. Some have thought the doxology of 4:11 would be a fitting close to the book, but other New Testament books include doxologies in the middle of the books. Since Christians in various regions are mentioned in the salutation, the possibility has been suggested that the book served as a cyclical letter. This possibility would explain the lack of personal greetings.

Themes of 1 Peter

The book reflects the message, *kerygma*, of the early church. Peter describes God as one who fulfills his promises (1:10-12). He describes the appearance of the Messiah (2:21-24) and Christ's resurrection and ascension (1:3, 21; 3:21, 22). Christ is coming to judge (1:7, 13; 4:5, 13; 5:1). These themes reflect the content of first-century preaching. The book has numerous references to God, Christ, and salvation.

The practical focus is seen in the emphasis on holy living (1:14-2:3), relationship to civil governments (2:13-17), the Christian home (3:1-7), and how to live right when persecuted for doing right (3:13-17; 4:13-16). Hope is a prominent theme. Themes that are woven into the book include persecution and suffering, holiness, the people of God, the example of Christ, submission, trials, injustice, and balanced Christian living.

Brief Outline of 1 Peter

1:1-2, Salutation

Part One
1:3-12, the blessings God has prepared for those who faithfully endure
1:13-25, a call to holy living, based on God's word, in the context of the church
2:1-3, a call to Christian maturity
2:4-10, a new identity for God's people

Part Two
2:11-12, live honorably as exiles
2:13-17, civic obligations
2:18-25, obligation of servants to endure as Christ endured
3:1-7, obligations in the home
3:8-12, obligations in daily relationships

Part Three
3:13-17, endurance in trials
3:18-22, Christ is the example of spiritual life
4:1-6, follow Christ's example
4:7-11, the ethical life
4:12-19, expect trials as a Christian
5:1-11, proper attitudes and conduct for various groups in the church
5:12-14, conclusion

Resources

The Greek text used is the 27th edition of *Novum Testamentus Graece* which is identical with the 4th revised edition of *The Greek New Testament*. Other tools I find helpful include my Greek concordance (Moulton and Geden), Greek lexicons (Arndt and Gingrich, and some older lexicons), and Greek vocabulary studies (*Theological Dictionary of the New Testament*; *Dictionary of New Testament Theology*, Colin Brown; and Moulton and Milligan).

Many English translations have been consulted. Those consulted most frequently include the English Standard Version (ESV), New English Translation (NET), and New International Version (NIV).

Various commentaries have been consulted. Those by Kelcy and Thompson have been especially helpful. I appreciate the studies prepared by Utley as they reflect my own training about how to approach the biblical text.

1 Peter 1

[Note: it is suggested that the student read the introductory materials in this guide before beginning any individual preparatory reading and analysis.]

CONTENT

The outline and paragraphing included in the Content section of each chapter are intended to serve only as suggestions or guides. The student is encouraged to read the text carefully and identify the paragraphs and subsections within each paragraph as part of his or her own study. The division of the biblical text into paragraphs is fairly standard in modern translations.

Outline of the Chapter
1:1-2	Salutation and greetings
1:3-12	A living hope and a tested faith
1:13-16	A call to holy living
1:17-21	The doctrinal foundations for faith and hope
1:22-25	How to live, based on God's enduring word

Note: in some outlines, this last paragraph continues through 2:3.

Overview of the Chapter

The primary purpose of the first section of 1 Peter is to comfort the exiled Christians in their suffering. This comfort is based on several truths: God has an eternal incontrovertible plan for his people, temporary trials prove the genuineness of faith, God's gracious plan for salvation extends beyond this world, God's word is certain.

Peter describes the salvation that God has prepared for his people (1:3-9). 1 Pet. 1:10-12 deals with the desire of the Old Testament prophets to understand the salvation that would be available in Christ. The prophets understood three things: the suffering of the Messiah, the glory that would follow, and that they were speaking of things to come after their own day.

A number of imperatives appear in the last half of the first chapter. Believers live out God's plan for them, even in the midst of sufferings, by girding their minds (1:13), being sober in spirit

(1:13), setting their hope on grace (1:13), not conforming to the present world (1:14), living holy lives (1:15), living reverently (1:17), and loving one another (1:22).

STUDY HELPS
1:1-2. Peter identifies himself as the author of the book. He uses the name Jesus gave him, Peter (Matt. 16:18). Paul most often calls him Cephas. The author identifies himself as Peter and as an apostle of Jesus Christ. In this description, he is identifying himself as one of the Twelve. A negative view of Peter is often included in sermons and classes, based on his denial of Jesus and his impetuous actions. In 1 Peter, we clearly see Peter's pastoral heart.

The recipients are aliens in five regions of Asia Minor. "Alien" refers to one who is living in an area that is not his or her homeland. The word "diaspora" (dispersion, scattering) usually referred to Jews who lived outside of Palestine. Here it refers to Christians in the churches, both Jews and Gentiles. "Alien" may include the idea that this world is not home for a Christian (1:17; 2:11). With the exception of Pontus, the locations mentioned were Roman provinces. Persons from some of these areas were present in Jerusalem on Pentecost (Acts 2:9-11).

1:2. Peter writes to those who are chosen or elect (v. 1). Three modifying phrases further describe the recipients. They are elect, (1) according to the foreknowledge of God the Father, (2) by the sanctification of the spirit, (3) unto obedience and sprinkling of the blood of Jesus Christ. The description as "elect exiles" could mean that God chose for them their present circumstances. Considering the spiritual focus of the descriptive, modifying phrases, and the context that follows, a more likely meaning is that "elect" refers to their status before God. Foreknowledge (*prognosis*, not the word used for predestination, used only here and in Acts 2:23) shows God the Father's sovereignty in the world.

"By the sanctification of the Spirit." They were elect through or because of the sanctification of the Holy Spirit. The consecration was done by the Holy Spirit. The New Testament uses the word "sanctify" to describe what happens at conversion. The Corinthians, despite their many problems, were sanctified

(1 Cor. 1:2; 6:11). The process of sanctification begins at conversion; the process must continue. Consecration and separation from the world, the practice of being set apart for a specific purpose, requires constant attention. Paul prays that the Thessalonians will be "wholly" sanctified (1 Thess. 5:23) which seems to point toward completeness, completely sanctified. Those who have experienced and are experiencing the sanctification of the Spirit are God's chosen ones.

"Unto obedience and sprinkling...." Unto (*eis*) means "for the purpose of." God has taken the initiative of choosing. God's people are chosen according to God's foreknowledge, by the sanctification of the Spirit, and for the purpose of obedience and sprinkling with the blood. God establishes the terms of the covenant; human beings must respond in obedience. "Of Jesus Christ" likely modifies both obedience and blood. Jesus' sacrifice must be appropriated. Jesus' sacrifice is effective for salvation when one becomes a Christian in baptism, but there is a need for continued application of the blood of Jesus throughout one's life (1 John 1:7). Sprinkling of blood was a part of receiving the Old Testament law (Exod. 24:7-8). The idea of sprinkling blood is used figuratively several times in the New Testament to refer to the power of Christ's blood in the daily Christian life, even as the priests in the Old Testament were sprinkled with sanctifying blood before serving (Heb. 9:15-23; 10:22; 12:24). Such figurative references, based in Old Testament practices, should not be considered strange in literature written to Jewish Christians. The reference to sprinkling blood has nothing to do with the practice of "sprinkling for baptism" that eventually developed in church history, many years after the New Testament practice of immersion was well-established.

"Grace and peace be multiplied." Grace and peace were commonly included in the greeting in Christian letters. Grace seems uniquely New Testament; peace is readily identified with the Old Testament. Here is one of the rare optative moods in the New Testament. The same word appears here, in 2 Pet. 1:2, and in Jude 2.

1:3-12. This description of God's plan to bless believers includes references to each person of the Godhead. "Blessed" is from the

Greek root where we get our word eulogy. The word "Lord" (*kurios*) is added to the compound name, Jesus Christ. The Jews used this word, "Lord," (Hebrew, *adon*) to refer to God because they did not want to pronounce the covenant name, YHWH, for fear of desecrating it or using it in vain. The New Testament authors used *kurios* to describe the deity of Christ. "Jesus is Lord" is a theologically rich affirmation that served as a public confession of faith, affirming the deity of Jesus. The contemporary church must learn to hear Jesus' deity in this phrase.

1:3-5. Several things are affirmed about God the Father. (1) According to his great mercy he gave us new birth, (a) into a living hope, (b) through the resurrection of Jesus Christ, (c) to an inheritance. These truths are for those who are guarded by God's power through faith for salvation. To be born again (*anagennao*, cf. 1 Pet. 1:23), has the same root as *gennao* in John 3:3. The new birth is a common description of the Christian conversion experience. This new birth is into a living hope and is through Jesus' resurrection. The result is an inheritance that is imperishable (*aphthartos*, without decay, incorruptible), undefiled (*amiantos*, unsoiled), and unfading (*amarantos*). The inheritance is reserved (*tereo*, to hold securely, as a military garrison) in heaven.

Not only is the inheritance reserved and held securely by God, the inheritance is for those who are protected (*phroureo*) by God. To know that God protects his people is especially important to those who are suffering and experiencing persecution. God's protective power operates through the faith of believers, pointing toward a salvation that is yet to be revealed in the last time. Salvation is a present reality that will one day be fully revealed. God guards the inheritance and protects the believer who is faithful. Utley describes the connection between God's part and the human part,

> It is the tension between these biblical dialectical pairs (i.e., God's sovereignty and human free will) which has caused the development of theological systems emphasizing only one side of the paradox. Both sides are biblical; both sides are necessary! God deals with humans by means of unconditional (God providing) and conditional (individuals responding) covenants.

1:6-7. What Peter has described in vv. 3-5 is cause for rejoicing, even though there is a brief and temporary time of various (*poikilos*) trials (*peirasmos*). Such trials are distressing, but the necessary result is the proving of our faith. The purpose (*hina*) clause says that the trials test and strengthen faith. The genuineness of faith is described as more precious than perishable gold. Gold is temporal, yet strong enough to be tested (*dokimazo*) by fire. The Christian faith is eternal, more precious, and equally strong under testing. Such authentic faith will result in praise, glory, and honor at the revelation (*apokalupsis*) of Jesus Christ. This word is not the common word for Jesus' coming, *parousia*. *Apokalupsis* says a time is coming when all will be disclosed and made known.

1:8-9. Jesus Christ is not seen or known at the present time. But without seeing him, we love him. The contrast is important. A time of revealing is coming, but faith sees and believes that which is not currently in view. By anticipating what is to come, rejoicing is possible in the present tense (v. 6) with an indescribable and glorious joy. The cause of joy is the certainty that you are receiving (*komizo*) the goal of your faith, even the salvation of your souls. Joy does not depend on external circumstances, but on knowing that God is working on our behalf. Sometimes in the New Testament, salvation is past tense (Rom. 8:24), sometimes it is ongoing (1 Cor. 1:18), and sometimes it is future, as in this passage. Salvation is sometimes described as glorification. Soul (*psuche*) refers to the entire person in this context.

1:10-12. God's actions and plan for our eternal salvation have been Peter's subject throughout the introduction and first part of the first chapter. "This salvation," based on God's preparations and protection, is a reality for God's people even in the midst of suffering. The Old Testament prophets spoke of God's grace by the Spirit of Christ within them. While we may think specifically of the prophets who wrote the books we know as Major Prophets and Minor Prophets, the Jews referred to the books we know as Books of History as the Former Prophets. The reference here is likely to numerous Old Testament writers. These "prophets" inquired diligently to identity a person and time, because they wanted to understand God's future plans for the salvation of his people. They wanted to understand the who and when of the coming of the Messiah. The text says that they desired a fuller understanding of three things: the sufferings of the Christ Messiah, the glories that would follow, and that the breadth of God's plan extended beyond themselves and the Jewish people. For a parallel use of "the glories," see 2 Pet. 2:10. "That they were not serving (*diakoneo*) themselves." This phrase may refer to the inclusion of the Gentiles in God's eternal plan. That the Messiah would come suffering and dying we now clearly see in Old Testament prophecy, but this was not the expectation of the Jews. They expected a military leader who would judge the nations and restore Israel to power.

In the preaching of the gospel through the Holy Spirit, these things have been announced to Peter's readers. The gospel is precious, not only because the prophets wanted to understand the things that are now being announced in the gospel, but because even angels long to look (*parakupto*, to stoop over to see more clearly, John 20:5, 11; James 1:25).

1:13-16. "Therefore" connects this paragraph to what has preceded it. In this case, the previous verses are the basis for the exhortations in vv. 13-16. Remember that Peter often intermingles doctrinal truths and practical applications. This passage contains a series of imperatives and participles. In this series of verbal forms, the participles have imperatival force.

The text literally reads, "Girding up the loins of your understanding." This phrase is a figure of speech that means to be prepared. NET, "Get your minds ready for action." The verb form is an aorist middle participle. Girding the loins, tucking the robe into the belt, was necessary for strenuous activity.

"Being sober." This present active participle indicates how to do the first action. This explains the translation, "by being sober." Being sober (*nepho*) refers to being alert and watchful. The sober person is balanced, steady, and self-restrained (cf. 4:7; 5:8). The relationship between this phrase and the previous phrase suggests that the sober mind can sensibly analyze situations and make wise decisions. Whether the adverb *teleios* belongs with sober or hope is not clear. NET translates "fully sober" and "set your hope completely."

"Put your hope completely in grace." This aorist active imperative reminds us that hope is based on God's nature and actions, not on life's circumstances. Grace was mentioned in v. 10 as the "coming grace." In this verse, grace will be fully known at the revelation of Jesus Christ. Hope is an essential part of endurance.

1:14. "Do not conform to the desires of your previous ignorance." One motivation for the changed life is that we are children of God who are now committed to obedience. The verb is a present participle. "As obedient children, not conforming...." The verb form which may be either present passive or present middle means either "not allowing yourselves to be shaped" or "not shaping yourselves." Both options remind us that salvation is a conditional covenant with a mandated human response, as is also the Christian life. The reference to previous desires and former ignorance fits Gentile readers better than Jewish readers.

1:15. "Become holy in all your conduct." A holy, set apart life, reflects the holy God who called us. "Become holy" is an aorist imperative. God's will for believers is holiness. Children reflect the nature of their parents. Holiness extends to every aspect of life, "in all your behavior (*anastrophe*)." The first part of 1 Peter confidently sets forth the heavenly goal, and then commands believers to live godly lives. Christianity is not an either-or, it is a both-and. Godly living—prepared minds, sober reflection, dependence on God's grace, rejecting the desires of the world—is not easy or automatic in the contemporary church that is surrounded by riches, tolerance for all kinds of thinking, and desires for independence and self-fulfillment.

1:16. The reason for the Christian's holiness is based on a quote from the Old Testament: You shall be holy for I am holy (Lev. 11:44-45, et.al.) Holiness, considering the Old Testament context, means "set apart to fulfill the covenant requirements."

1:17-21. A casual reading of this paragraph suggests that one is reading doctrinal teaching. What is God like? What should one understand about redemption, Jesus' sacrifice, God's eternal plan, Jesus' resurrection and glory? Filling one's mind with such thoughts motivates our actions and makes certain our faith and hope in God.

1:17. The first class condition can be translated as fact. "Since you address...." To the believer, God is Father and God is impartial judge of the work or actions of each person. Each person can choose a course of action regarding a relationship with God. Because each person has a choice, believers conduct themselves with fear (*phobos*, reverence may better catch the meaning in the context) during their temporary sojourn (*paroikia*). This word is different from the "exile" of 1:1. Here the reference is to the believer's time on earth. Sojourn means to live in a place that is not home, a description of the Christian's time spent on earth.

1:18-19. Christians confidently conduct themselves with reverence because of what they know about Christ and their redemption. Verses 18-21 may be an early hymn or creed. The use of such literature is well-known in various New Testament texts (Phil. 2:6-11; Col. 1:15-16; 1 Tim. 3:16; 2 Tim. 2:11-13). The use of the verb form "to redeem" (*lutroo*) is not common in the New Testament. It is used only here and in Luke 24:21 and Tit. 2:14. Christ as our redemption is a common New Testament theme. The readers were redeemed from empty conduct (*anastrophe*) by the blood of Christ, not with perishable things. The empty life was inherited from their forefathers. This description may refer to Old Testament traditions, or it may refer to past immoral practices (1:14). The blood of Christ is described as the "precious blood as of a lamb." The price for redemption was the blood of Christ, unblemished (*amomos*) and spotless (*aspilos*). These adjectives indicate that Christ was a holy sacrifice. Other New Testament passages describe Jesus as the Lamb who removes the sin of the world (e.g. John 1:29).

1:20. "He (Christ) was foreknown before the foundation of the world." The death of Jesus was a part of God's eternal plan. God did not have to develop Plan B because the Jews had rejected Jesus. Jesus' death was not an afterthought or a change in God's eternal plan. God's Messiah came to earth to die. The reference to "Christ known before the foundation of the world" speaks to his preexistence. In the last times he has appeared for the sake of the believers.

1:21. "You," the last word in v. 20, is modified by v. 21. "You, the ones through him believing in God who raised him from the dead and gave him glory, so that your faith and hope are in God."

1:22-25. The Greek language loves to pile up participles. Verse 22 says, "Having purified your souls by obedience of the truth." The verbs in the paragraph can be connected in various ways. Many participial phrases are best translated as main verbs, as in my translation below.

1:22-23. "You have purified your souls by obedience of the truth to have sincere brotherly love. With pure hearts love one another earnestly. You have been born anew not by perishable seed but by imperishable, through the living and enduring word of God."

Obedience (1:2, 14, 22) is a part of the Christian life. This reference makes clear that obedience is "of the truth." Obedience is connected to purifying the soul. Souls are purified by obeying the truth. The reference is not to meritorious salvation that earns God's grace, but to covenant faithfulness that is essential to holy (set-apart) living. While the connection may not be clear to us, the text says that one result of obedience is genuine brotherly love. Since such love is the evidence and product of obedience, the readers are commanded (imperative) to love one another intently (*ektenos*).

1:23. You have been born again (*anagennao*, born again, perfect passive participle, see 1:3 where the same word is used). The new birth is not by corruptible seed, but by the incorruptible seed which is the living and enduring word of God. The new birth is through the preaching of God's word, the gospel (1:12).

1:24-25. These verses contain a quotation from Isa. 40:6-8 LXX. God's word is eternal even though human existence is finite. The word that was preached to Peter's readers was the enduring and forever word of the Lord. Two different Greek words are available for "word." The use of *logos* in 1:23 and *rhema* in 1:25 does not seem to point to a significant interpretative point. In this context, the words seem synonymous, describing God's revelation.

1 Peter 2

[Note: it is suggested that the student read the introductory materials in this guide before beginning any individual preparatory reading and analysis.]

CONTENT
The outline and paragraphing included in the Content section of each chapter are only suggestions or guides. The student is encouraged to read the text carefully and identify the paragraphs and subsections within each paragraph as part of his or her own study. In this chapter, the division of the biblical text into paragraphs is fairly standard in modern translations.

Outline of the Chapter
2:1-3	Admonition to Christian growth
2:4-10	A chosen living stone and a chosen holy nation
2:11-12	Live as God's servants
2:13-17	Submit to civil authorities
2:18-25	The submission of slaves, and the example of Christ's suffering

Overview of the Chapter
      The first part of the chapter concludes the first section of 1 Peter (1:2-2:10). The transitional verses in 2:11-12 provide a kind of hinge upon which the book turns and unfolds. The second part of the book (2:13-3:12) focuses on the appropriate Christian response in a variety of life settings and relationships.

      In this chapter, Peter uses numerous metaphors: newborn babies, 2:1; living stones, 2:5; priesthood, 2:9; people, 2:9; aliens and strangers, 2:11; sheep, 2:25.

STUDY HELPS
2:1-3. "Therefore" (*oun*) provides a connection with the previous chapter but also begins a new exhortation. These verses are

treated as a separate paragraph in this study to honor the chapter divisions and assist the student in using this Bible Study Guide.

"Putting to one side (*apotithemi*) all evil (*kakia*), all deceit (*dolos*) and hypocrisy (*hupokrisis*) and envy (*phthonos*), and all slander (*katalalia*), yearn for (*epipotheo*) the unadulterated (*adolos*) milk that is rational and reasonable (*logikos*, related to the word) so in it you will increase (*auxano*, grow) unto salvation, if you have tasted that the Lord is kind (*chrestos*, gracious)." "Yearn for" is the principal verb in the extended sentence of vv. 1-3.

Putting aside is an aorist participle. The aorist often indicates a total once-and-for-all action. The Greek word, *apotithemi*, is frequently used in the Bible to describe the process of getting rid of a prior way of life (Eph. 4:22, 25, 31; Col. 3:8; Heb. 12:1). The things to be discarded are placed in three groups, each preceded by "all." Evil is sometimes translated malice. Deceit means to entrap by trickery. Slander is literally "speaking against."

"As newborn babies" is not a description of the Christians but is a modifier of the verb. To think that all of the Christians to whom Peter was writing were new Christians would be to draw an incorrect conclusion. What kind of yearning should every Christian have for pure reasonable nourishment, nourishment that comes from the word of God (1:23-25)? The yearning is like the strong desire of a newborn baby who desires to suckle at the mother's breast. Such yearning is necessary for both new Christians and Christians who have years of experience in the faith. Such yearning leads to spiritual maturity. Spiritual maturity is not automatic for the Christian. The pure milk is unadulterated (*adolos*), an adjective that is basically the same word as deceit in 2:1 (*dolos*), only with the alpha privative (which serves as a negative) attached. The word of God is essential to the new birth (1:23); the word is essential to Christian growth (2:2). The concept of a Christian who does not read and seek to understand the Bible is an oxymoron. "If you have tasted" is a first class condition, a statement of fact, thus "because you have tasted the graciousness of the Lord."

2:4-10. These verses contain a new thought. "To whom coming...you are built up." "Whom" refers to the Lord, the last word of v. 3 in Greek. The present participle (coming) is likely not an imperative, but rather expresses the natural result of understanding God's kindness. "As you come to him, you are built up...." Peter changes the metaphor in v. 4. In the new metaphor, the Lord (Jesus) is as a living stone rejected by men. Christians come to the living stone. The metaphor will be expanded to reflect the rejected building stone (Ps. 118:22), a stone of stumbling (Isa. 8:14-15), and possibly the kingdom stone of Dan. 2:45. The rejected stone is in fact chosen and precious for God. The rejected stone is disapproved (*apodokimazo*, tested and discarded) by men.

2:5. Peter's readers come to the Lord as living stones to be built into a spiritual house, to become a holy priesthood to offer spiritual sacrifices. The spiritual house results in a holy priesthood. Here the church is being described in Old Testament terminology. The holy priesthood offers spiritual sacrifices acceptable to God through Jesus Christ (cf. Rom. 12:1-2).

2:6-8. In all of these references, Peter sees the fulfillment of Scripture. He cites portions of Isa. 28:16; Ps. 118:22; and Isa. 8:14 to explain vv. 4-5. In order to connect the citations, Peter writes that believers share the honor, but disbelievers stumble, unto which they were appointed (*tithemi*). The text in v. 7 literally reads, "to you who believe is the value (*time*)." Is Christ precious (*time*), or are the readers being counted of value? I prefer to understand the value that God places upon believers, a value they share with Christ. Two contrasts are presented in the context: (1) the Christians are despised foreigners in the view of the world, but of value to God, and (2) Christ as the stone rejected by men is valued by believers. In v. 8, Peter writes that the unbelievers stumble, disobeying the word, to which they were appointed. Peter is not describing predestination. They were not destined to disobey. The simple truth is this: the natural result of disobeying the word is stumbling.

2:9-10. "But you" (plural) provides a contrast to the unbelievers of v. 8. The descriptions Peter uses are allusions to Old Testament descriptions of God's people (e.g. Ex. 19:5-6; Dt. 7:6; Isa. 43:20-21). The church is chosen by God. The church as a royal priesthood is called to provide people access to God. The church is chosen race (*genos*, translated as 'family' in Acts 7:13; 13:26), holy nation, God's treasured possession (Ex. 19:5; Tit. 2:14). This identity enables the church to "proclaim (*exaggello*, declare, only here in the New Testament) the virtues (*arete*, excellence) of the one who called you out of darkness into his marvelous light." God's people as God's representative holy nation are chosen and equipped to proclaim God and help people find access to God.

Martin Luther coined the phrase "the priesthood of the believers." The individualism and independence of Western thought has turned this into personal freedom—focused on individual beliefs and lifestyle preferences. The word "priesthood" is a collective noun; the biblical concept is corporate. Plural pronouns are used in vv. 5, 7 and 9. This passage is proclamation-focused for the corporate body of believers. It is not focused on personal freedom to approach God outside the context of the believing body. While it is true that each Christian has direct access to God, that is not the point of this passage. The work of a priest is not to access God for personal benefit. Priests provide a bridge between needy people and a holy God. Priests connect people to God, both God's people and unbelievers. Priests proclaim and present the word of God or they are not priests (cf. Mal. 2:7).

2:10. In this verse are quotations from Hosea 1:10 and 2:23. Peter's point is based on the names of Hosea's children. Those who were not God's people are now God's people; those who had not received mercy have now received mercy. The context seems to suggest a reference to the inclusion of the Gentiles, a natural follow-up to the responsibility to proclaim God's mercy, a responsibility that Israel was given in the Old Testament toward the nations.

2:11-12. These two verses serve as a transition to the second part of the book (see the outline in the Introduction). As such they serve as a hinge connecting the two sections. Whereas the first section of the book was largely didactic, the second section of 1 Peter is more practical and is characterized by various terms of address—beloved, slaves, wives, husbands, all.

2:11. Verse 11 begins with a term of address, "beloved." "As aliens (*paroikos*, see 1:17 for a related noun form) and strangers (*parepidemos*), keep yourselves away from fleshly desires that war against the soul." Christians are not at home in the world. The words used suggest that Christians are residents of another realm. Christians face a constant struggle with the desires and realities that are part of life in this world.

2:12. "Keeping your conduct (*anastrophe*, 1:15,18) good among the Gentiles." The participle functions as an imperative. Good conduct is an antidote. "In whatsoever things they malign you as wrongdoers, they seeing (*epopteuo*) your good works will glorify God in the day when he visits." Church history tells us that Christians were at times accused of cannibalism, incest, atheism, treason, and immorality. When unbelievers see the good works of Christians, they will glorify God. Our lives point toward God. "Gentiles" refers to the unbelievers among whom Peter's readers were living.

Visitation (*episcope*) refers to God drawing near. Some take this to refer to the end of the world and God's final judgment. God's presence can signify either blessing or judgment. Visitation is not a word usually used with reference to Jesus' coming (*parousia*, presence, or *apokalupsis*, appearing). The word visitation is used in a positive sense in Lk. 1:68; 7:16; 19:44. The interpretation of the verse does not depend on which option is chosen. In whatever day of God's visitation, God will be glorified by unbelievers because of the life of the believers.

2:13-17. This paragraph contains a series of instructions about how to live in the world. In the contemporary world where civil disobedience is popular, the church and believers would do well to hear Peter's description of civil obedience. "Submit" (*hupotasso*) is an aorist imperative. Submission is a choice. Submission is a theme in 1 Peter (2:13, 18; 3:1, 5, 22; 5:5). Submission for the Lord's sake bases our submission on the Lord's will and example. Peter urges submission to "every human creation" meaning everything instituted by human beings, referring primarily to governments. Peter's examples include the king and his governors. The king is supreme (*hupoecho*) and he sends governors to punish evil-doers and praise right-doers. Governments have this authority from God (Rom. 13:4).

2:15. God desires the submission of his people because by doing right they will silence (*phimoo*, literally, to muzzle, but used figuratively here) the ignorance of foolish persons. This clearly repeats the thought of 2:12 where uninformed persons are accusing believers without cause.

2:16. This sentence has no main verb; the verb "to live" may be understood. "Live as free people, but not as having your freedom as a pretext for evil, rather as slaves of God." We Christians easily justify our bad behaviors on the basis of what we experience in the world. We sometimes omit "good-doing" from our lives in times of turmoil, persecution, criticism and rejection. The instructions of this paragraph were especially significant for first-century Christians who were the outcasts of society and were suffering at the hands of the Roman government. Believers who have been freed from sin are freed to serve God (Rom. 6:16-23). Freedom is not cause for license (Gal. 5:13).

2:17. Four imperatives conclude the paragraph. Honor all people; love the brotherhood (*adelphotes*); fear God; honor the king. The first and last verbs in the series are the same (*timao*, to honor). The command to love the brotherhood points back to 1:22. To fear (*phobeo*) God may include being fearful or afraid, but a common New Testament meaning is "reverence, awe and respect." To submit to and honor the king is an especially impressive instruction when one considers that Nero was the Roman emperor (AD 54-68).

2:18-25. This section begins with a direct address, "slaves." The Greek word is *oiketes* (household servants), not *doulos* (slaves). While the New Testament uses the word "slaves" to refer to all Christians in their relationship to God, one must distinguish references to literal slaves from figurative uses that refer to all Christians. In 2:18, the reference is to household servants, to be followed by more household instructions to the wives (3:1) and the husbands (3:7). The observation that the master-servant relationship of the first century may be approximately parallel to the employer-employee relationship today has merit, and may help with understanding the application of these instructions in some modern-day circumstances.

Servants are to be submissive to their masters with all respect (*phobos*, fear; see 2:17). Believing servants respect their masters "for the Lord's sake" (because they respect God). The participle is used as a command. This instruction contains elements from the previous paragraph. Servants are obligated not only to good and gentle masters, but also to those who are perverse (*skolios*, crooked).

2:19-20. "For this [is] grace" means that this pleases God: "when (first class condition) a Christian suffers unjustly but for conscience toward God endures sorrows (*lupe*)." What praise is there when one sins, is mistreated, and endures patiently? But when one does good, suffers, and endures patiently, this [is] grace with God. The last phrase in v. 20 is repeated from the first phrase in v. 19.

2:21-25. These verses may be a poem. The literal translation given here maintains the original word order and shows parallel constructions.

For to this you were called,
That also Christ suffering for you
To you leaving an example
In order that you might follow in the steps of him,
    Who sin did not do
    Neither was found deceit in the mouth of him,
Who being reviled not he reviled back,
Suffering he did not threaten,
But he committed himself to the one judging justly;
    Who himself carried our sins
    In his body on the tree,
    So that the sins renouncing
    In righteousness we might live,
    By whose wounds we are healed.
For you were as sheep wandering.

2:21. "Unto this were you called." The text is best understood by reading "this" as a reference to what is to come, not to what has gone before. Believers are called to imitate Jesus in his submissiveness, suffering, lack of deceit, lack of threats, and sacrifice. That believers are called to submission, suffering, and self-sacrifice is not a popular theme today. Christ's suffering is an example for Christians to follow. If Christ's suffering is the specific example given for me as I follow in his steps, what does that imply for my imitation of Christ? If Christians are called to follow Christ in suffering, how much suffering should I expect? Could it ever be true that a Christian would not suffer?

2:22-23. In the context of 2:18-25, Jesus is presented as our example of suffering because he suffered unjustly. He did not suffer for his own sins; in fact, he committed no sin. He did not suffer for his own wrongdoing; he did not speak with deceit, reproach, or threats. He suffered, all the while entrusting himself to the just judge. The description of Jesus in 2:22-25 contains wording similar to Isaiah 53.

The Use of Isaiah 53 in 1 Peter 2:21-25
2:22 Nor was deceit found in his mouth, Isa. 53:9
2:24 He himself bore our sins, Isa. 53:4, 12
2:24 By his wound you were healed, Isa. 53:5
2:25 Going astray like sheep, Isa. 53:6

2:24. Jesus suffered, not because he was bearing his own sins, but because he was bearing our sins in his physical body on the cross. Jesus died in our stead so that we could be disconnected from sin (*apoginomai*, to be separated, apart from, thus to be deceased or to renounce). In this verse is the only occurrence of this verb in the New Testament. Being separated from sin is an important prerequisite to living in righteousness. The healing mentioned is spiritual healing, metaphorically referring to salvation. Jesus' suffering is summarized in the mention of the wounds he suffered.

2:25. As already mentioned, the extended passage in vv. 22-25 alludes to Isaiah 53 several times. As sheep stray, so people stray from God. On the basis of Jesus' suffering, "you have now returned...." Jesus is described as a shepherd (*poimen*, often translated pastor in other contexts) and guardian (*episkopos*, often translated overseer or bishop in other contexts) of the soul. Peter will use both of these concepts again in 1 Pet. 5:1-3 to describe church leaders.

1 Peter 3

[Note: it is suggested that the student read the introductory materials in this guide before beginning any individual preparatory reading and analysis.]

CONTENT

The outline and paragraphing included in the Content section of each chapter are only suggestions or guides. The student is encouraged to identify the paragraphs and subsections within each paragraph as part of his or her own study. The division of the biblical text into paragraphs is generally standardized in modern translations.

Outline of the Chapter
3:1-7   Instructions to wives and husbands
3:8-12   Instructions for all
3:13-17   Suffering for doing right
3:18-22   The example of Christ's suffering and God's plan
   Note: some translations extend the paragraph through 4:6.

Overview of the Chapter

The first part of the chapter concludes instructions for Christians living in an alien world. To the instructions of Chapter 2, instructions directed to "beloved ones" and to "servants," are added sections concerning "wives" (3:1-6), "husbands" (3:7), and "all of you" (3:8-12). Such instructions were common in first century literature, usually beginning with those who were considered weakest in society. In 1 Peter, the order is servants, wives, husbands.

The primary theme of the second part of the chapter, beginning at 3:13, concerns how one should understand the presence of suffering when one is doing right. This theme was introduced in 2:18-25 and is expanded in 3:13-4:19.

The chapter contains a difficult passage beginning in 3:18, and this Bible Study Guide will depart from its normal

STUDY HELPS

3:1-7. "Likewise" points back to the admonition to "beloved ones" (2:13) and to "servants" (2:18). "You wives, be submissive to your own husbands...." The participle has imperatival force. The goal of submission is to gain (*kerdaino*) the unbelieving husband. The first class condition means that the situation described actually existed. Some Christian wives had husbands who were disobedient to the word (cf. 2:8). The wife by her submissive spirit could possibly gain her husband by her example, not by "preaching" to him the word, but "without a word." Lifestyle and behavior are often more powerful than the words that are spoken. The husbands would be gained as they observed (*epopteuo,* repeated from 2:12) pure (*hagnos*) and reverent (*phobos,* fear) conduct (*anastrophe,* repeated from 2:12). *Epoptueo* can be used to refer to eyewitnesses. Here is a good example of the use of *phobos* (literally, fear) to mean "reverent." The goal of the Christian example is evangelism.

3:3-4. The beauty (*cosmos*, compare our word cosmetics) of the wives is not to be external, in braiding hair, wearing gold, or putting on clothes, but [the beauty is in] the hidden person (*anthropos*, literally "man") of the heart, in an ever present, humble and peaceable spirit, which in the presence of God is very valuable (*poluteles*, costly, extremely expensive). Beauty is internal, not external. The external adornments that are mentioned most likely refer to expensive and elaborate fashions of the first century, which things brought social acceptance and rank. A modern application of these verses could apply to both women and men. Some people choose to "dress up;" others choose to "dress down." In both cases, one is trying to say something about oneself by one's method of dress, something that is prohibited by this passage. Let the things that declare who we and give us our identity in Christ be internal. The internal beauty that Peter describes is imperishable (*aphthartos*, incorruptible, which I translated as "ever present"). The same word was used in 1:4 to describe the heavenly inheritance and in 1:23 to describe the seed of God's word.

3:5-6. "In this way," by being submissive to their own husbands and with internal beauty, the holy women who hoped in God adorned themselves. The Greek adverb *pote* is translated "long ago, then, in former times." As Sarah obeyed Abraham, calling him lord, whose children (daughters) you have become by doing right and not fearing (*phobeo*) any terror (*ptosesis*, alarm).

3:7. "Likewise the husbands, dwelling together according to knowledge, as with a weaker female vessel, giving (*aponemo*) honor as also heirs together of the grace of life, so as not to be hindered (*egkopto*, literally cut down, frustrated) your prayers." This more literal translation does not read smoothly in English, but it catches some subtle nuances of the Greek text. "According to knowledge" is usually translated "with understanding or consideration." Knowledge was also used with reference to intimacy. "Weaker vessel" may refer to social status or to physical strength; in the context the former is preferable. "Vessel" refers to a helpful instrument or equipment but is used figuratively here. Given the Old Testament context of the passage and the reference to Sarah and Abraham, I like to note that the woman complements and completes the abilities of the man (Genesis 2). See also my comments on 1 Thess. 4:3-6 and 4:7-8, where the reference to "one's vessel" is to one's body (not one's wife) and the need to pursue holiness by avoiding any and all kinds of sexual liberties.

The husband should give honor to his wife because she is also an heir of the grace of life. "Grace of life" is usually interpreted as a reference to eternal life, but see also 2:19-20, where God's favor (*charis*, grace) in this life is the result of enduring unjust suffering. In the first century, the possibility that a Christian would be called to suffer injustice equally applied to men and women, or in the context of 2:19-20, to both male and female servants. The point is that men and women are equally heirs of God's grace and favor. The last phrase in v. 7 is easy to understand but hard to apply. In what way are a husband's prayers "cut off"? While the phrase may modify both participles in the verse (dwelling together, giving honor), it more naturally connects with the second participle. Honoring one's wife as one who shares God's grace strengthens a husband's prayers. The process of honoring and sharing life with my wife who is also a sister in Christ makes my prayers stronger. When I do not give her that honor, my prayers are frustrated.

3:8-12. "Finally, for everyone." The sentence has no main verb; "to be" is understood. Be harmonious (*homophrone*, literally, of the same mind), sympathetic (*sumpathes*, suffering together), affectionate (*philadelphos*), compassionate, humble. The sentence continues, "not returning evil...but blessing...because you were called to inherit a blessing (*eulogia*)." Not returning evil or insult suggests forgiveness.

3:10-12. These verses are a quotation from Psalm 34:12-16. The passage has three admonitions: keep the tongue, turn from evil, seek and pursue peace. Verse 12 says that the Lord notices and hears the righteous and opposes the wicked. Lord is a reference to YHWH. This paragraph concludes the second part of the book.

3:13-17. The theme of the third section of the book of 1 Peter is suffering. This paragraph introduces the theme by noting that the Christian at times suffers for doing what is right. The rhetorical answer of v. 13 anticipates a negative response. In most cases, no one is working to hurt those who are zealous (*zelotes*, zealots, followers) of what is good. Yet, in some cases followers of what is good receive evil. This idea provides the transition to v. 14.

3:14. But if you suffer for righteousness, you are blessed. The suffering mentioned in v. 14 is not common, but it is possible. The meaning is that examples of suffering for righteousness would be limited in number. The blessing mentioned is the same word that is used in the Sermon on the Mount (*makarios*). Do not fear (*phobeo*) the fear (*phobos*) they cause, do not be troubled (*tarasso*). Here the Greek phrase, "fear of them," likely means the fear they are associated with, thus, the fear they cause. The Christian rests secure in the midst of life's circumstances through confidence in the Lord.

3:15. "Sanctify (*hagiazo*, set apart, aorist imperative) Christ as Lord." The use of the word "Lord" with reference to God the Father throughout this chapter suggests that 3:15 is an affirmation of the deity of Christ. Decisions about how one will respond to Christ are made in the "heart," a word that is used at times to refer to the mind, and at other times to refer to the entire person. In the context, both ideas make sense. The Christian demonstrates the belief that Christ is Lord through actions. "Always ready for a defense *(apologia)* to everyone who asks you for an account concerning the hope in you." *Apologia* could mean a legal defense, as in a courtroom. Christians know how to respond to those who question the reason for their hope.

3:16. Where the sentence division should occur is in question. Does the phrase "with gentleness and respect *(phobos)*" describe how to present one's defense, or does it describe the behavior of the person slandered so that those who accuse are put to shame? Christians must always act in accordance with their own consciences. This statement reflects the meaning of "good conscience" (see 2:19; 3;16,21).

3:17. It is better to suffer for doing good than for doing evil. "If God wills it," the fourth class condition suggests that such is far outside of what is to be expected.

3:18-22. "Because" *(oti)* connects v. 18 with the preceding paragraph. The truthfulness of verses 13-17—and especially v. 17, that God's will may include suffering for those who do good—is affirmed by the suffering and death of Christ.

If one jumps from 3:18 to 4:1 in the reading, the text still makes good sense. A first step toward understanding the text and the illustration that Peter uses is to ask the question, "What is Peter's point?" In the immediate context, how a mention of Noah, the ark, and baptism advances the argument is unclear. The answer to the question lies not in the illustration but in the larger context that surrounds the illustration. Peter is saying that unjust suffering can only be understood by keeping one's eyes focused on spiritual things. Christ's death in the flesh was important; his being made alive in the spirit was even more important. This focus is seen with the repeated use of "the flesh" (3:18, 21; 4:1, 2, 6), a repetition that is not apparent in all translations.

3.18. The thought being conveyed in the verse is this: "You know that vv. 13-17 are true because at one time Christ also suffered, because of sin (not his own), the just for the unjust, in order to bring you to God."

Christ's once-for-all suffering and death for sins is an example of injustice, the just for the unjust, to bring you to God. A textual variant in v. 18 forces one to decide whether the verb should be "suffered" or "died." The external evidence better fits "died" but "suffered" better fits the context and the intended link with v. 17 by the use of both *oti* (because, for) and *kai* (also) in v. 18. In the New Testament, "to suffer" appears alongside "sin" in only one other place, but that place is 1 Pet. 4:1. "Suffered" is preferred in the context. Several other textual variants are found in the verse but do not alter the meaning of the text.

Christ suffered to bring you to God by, on the one hand (*men*) having been put to death in the flesh, on the other hand (*de*) having been made alive in the spirit. The phrase "in the flesh" appears numerous times in the paragraph that extends through 4:6. Because spirit and flesh are set in opposition to one another, as are life and death, the reference is to the human spirit rather than to the Holy Spirit. The contrast is between physical existence and spiritual existence. Christ was put to death in the flesh, that is, in relation to his physical existence. Christ was made alive in the spirit, that is, in relation to his spiritual existence.

Verse 18 presents the theme thought of this section, vv. 19-21a function parenthetically with an illustration that is based on type and antitype. The type is described in vv. 19-20, the antitype is in v. 21a. Verses 21b-22 return to the theme thought.

3:19-20. These verses contain an explanation of the type that corresponds to the antitype in v. 21a. "In which (his spiritual existence) he went and made proclamation (*kerusso*) to the spirits in prison." The use of the verb "went" (*poreuomai*, depart, go, go away, go forth, go up) should be noted. *Kerusso* means to proclaim or announce. The use of a different verb to describe the declaration—not the verb *euaggelizo* which means to preach the gospel—is noteworthy. Jesus, in his spiritual existence, made proclamation to spirits in prison, but his proclamation was not gospel proclamation. The word "now" does not appear in the original text and is unnecessary.

A more literal reading helps catch the message: "It was in the spirit (his spiritual existence) that he "went" and made a proclamation to the imprisoned spirits. They (the spirits) were disobedient at some time or other. After that, the longsuffering of God endured in the days of Noah as an ark was being constructed. In that ark a few, that is, eight souls, were saved through water."

Two theories that have been advanced concerning the teaching of this text are these: (1) he preached to the spirits of men who had died (see Heb. 12:23 for a use of the word "spirit" referring to human beings), or (2) he preached to evil angels (2 Pet. 2:4-5; Jude 6). Several things in the passage are clearly stated: Jesus had been made alive in the spirit, he "went" and "made a proclamation" to spirits in prison, those spirits were formerly disobedient at some time, later God was longsuffering in Noah's time when the ark was constructed. Whether one opts for proclamation to those human beings who were disobedient while Noah was building the ark, or to fallen angels who sinned before Noah's day, the questions remain as to why and what and when Jesus proclaimed.

The spirits to whom Jesus made proclamation were those who disobeyed then (*pote*), at some time in the past. The patience of God waited in the days of Noah while the ark was being built.

Four possibilities have been advanced to explain the statements of vv. 19-20.

- The preexistent Christ, before the Incarnation, proclaimed "in the spirit" through Noah to the people of Noah's day, those people who were in Peter's day spirits imprisoned, possibly by death or by their disobedience (cf. 1:11; 2 Pet. 2:5).
- Christ, between his death and resurrection, "in the spirit" went and proclaimed to the people of Noah's day, possibly proclaiming his victory or pronouncing blessings on Noah and his family.

- Christ, between his death and resurrection, "in the spirit" went and proclaimed to the angels who were imprisoned, possibly announcing his victory.
- Christ, having been resurrected (made alive) and victorious in his Ascension, declared his victory to the imprisoned angels.

Perhaps those to whom Peter was writing understood exactly what Peter was saying. That we struggle to determine exactly what occurred does not mean we cannot understand Peter's point. (See comments on 3:21-22.)

The illustration, expanding the description of the antitype, continues with another mention of the ark, the next event after Noah was building the ark. In the ark, eight persons were saved (*diasozo*, preserved, delivered) through (*dia*) water. The compound verb (*dia* + *sozo*) is not unusual when the following prepositional phrase is governed by the same preposition (*dia*). The text says that these eight were saved in the ark through water.

3:21. "Which also to you is an antitype—baptism now saves (*sozo*)." The antitype is that which corresponds to the type. The type is a representation or copy, the antitype is the real thing. Here is the key to understanding the passage. The type is found in vv. 19-20, the antitype is found in v. 21a. The significance of baptism is not physical; it is not removing the dirt of the flesh. The significance of baptism is spiritual (in the spiritual existence realm), the response to God of a good conscience. Baptism saves through the resurrection (*anastasis*, making alive) of Jesus Christ. Resurrection connects with "made alive" in v. 18. Baptism declares Jesus' death, burial, and resurrection. Baptism declares the death of the old person and the new life in the spirit. This contrast between suffering and death "in the flesh" and life "in the spirit" focuses Peter's primary point. In the contrast, one understands how God works his eternal will through temporary circumstances during our time "in the flesh."

3:22. This Jesus who suffered in the flesh and was made alive in the spirit is at God's right hand. His ascension to heaven is described with the verb "went," the same verb as was used in v. 19. Having submitted himself to God's will, angels, authorities and powers (all descriptions of spiritual beings, spirits) have been made subject to him.

Of the four options presented earlier, the option that best seems to fit the text is the fourth. Jesus proclaimed his victory to the imprisoned spirits after his ascension. The proclamation was made after his return to heaven. He was made alive (resurrected), he "went" (the same verb is used in v. 19 and v. 22) referring to the Ascension, and he proclaimed his victory to the spirits who were now subject to him. This description honors the connection between vv. 18-19 and v. 21b-22, paying close attention to the parallels.

Note: the paragraph continues in 4:1-6, but to maintain the chapter divisions and the ease of use of this Bible Study Guide, the comments on the rest of the paragraph appear in the next chapter.

1 Peter 4

[Note: it is suggested that the student read the introductory materials in this guide before beginning any individual preparatory reading and analysis.]

CONTENT

The outline and paragraphing included in the Content section of each chapter are only suggestions or guides. The student is encouraged to read the text carefully and identify the paragraphs and subsections within each paragraph as part of his or her own study.

Outline of the Chapter
4:1-6   "Suffering in the flesh" has changed our lives
4:7-11   Be good managers of God's gifts
4:12-19   Suffering as a Christian

Overview of the Chapter

    This chapter continues Peter's emphasis on suffering as a Christian. The paragraph that began in 3:18 is continued in 4:1-6. Peter describes how the "in the spirit" reality of a Christian changes the "in the flesh" experience.

    The second part of the chapter sets forth the implications and application of vv. 1-6. Because Christians are committed to living according to God, they pursue a different lifestyle in the context of the mutual faith of the believers (vv. 7-11).

    Peter concludes the chapter by returning to the subject of suffering. Trials are to be expected, but God is present to bless his people in the midst of trials and suffering. Suffering as a Christian is not shameful but is necessary. Suffering results in glory to God as the Christian trusts God and continues to do what is good.

STUDY HELPS

4:1-6. "Therefore" or "then" links these verses to 3:18-22. The link between 3:18 and 4:1 is made more apparent by seeing 3:19-22 as a parenthesis or illustration. Since Christ has suffered in the flesh (cf. 3:18), Christians must be prepared for the same experience. "In the flesh" refers to physical life in this world. The focus is not on sinful desires ("Do not walk according to the flesh," Gal. 5), but on physical existence. Jesus was human; he died for us. Because he suffered, we can expect suffering. We are to arm ourselves (*hoplizo*, to equip) with the same attitude (*ennoia*, understanding, intent, mind), that is, with the attitude of Christ, because the one who has suffered in the flesh has ceased (*pauo*) from sin. Christians who are made alive spiritually have died to sin and are done with sin (Rom. 6:7, 11). Jesus died so we could cease from sinning (2:24). Believers who follow Christ's example of suffering will also follow his example of victory over sin.

4:2. "Thus to live the rest of the time in the flesh no longer for the desires of men but for the will of God." The phrase, "in the flesh," is a description of physical life in this context. The connection between v. 2 and v. 1 has been the subject of much discussion. Should v. 2 be understood as modifying "ceasing from sin" or as modifying the main verb, "arm yourselves"? Does the "*eis*" clause communicate purpose or result? The preferred understanding is that Christians arm themselves in order to (purpose) live for the will of God.

4:3. The time that has passed was sufficient to do the will of the Gentiles, journeying in various sins. Gentiles metaphorically refers to unbelievers. This verse describes a previous life spent in sensuality and paganism. The list of sins includes sensuality (*aselgeia*), lust (*epithumia*), drunkenness (*oinophlugia*), carousing (*komos*), banqueting with drinking, idolatry, immorality (*potos*), and abominable idolatries. This list includes some of the most common sins associated with the pagan world.

4:4-5. "By which they are astonished that you do not rush with them into the same excesses of license, and they blaspheme you." This verse explains again the accusations of the unbelievers against the Christians (cf. 2:23, 25; 3:16). They (the unbelievers) will give account to the one who is ready to judge the living and the dead, referring to all human beings.

4:6. This verse does not reflect the same preaching as 3:18. The verb in 3:18 means to proclaim or announce. The verb in 4:6 means gospel preaching that was presented to certain people who are now dead, although the preaching was done while they were alive. The dead who are mentioned appear to be those who responded to the gospel before they died. The focus is not on the "who" of the preaching but on the "purpose" of the preaching. The purpose of preaching is that while human beings are being judged in the flesh according to men, they may live in the spirit according to God.

With the repetition of the phrases "in the flesh" and "in the spirit," the argument Peter has been advancing is concluded. To summarize 3:18-4:6 briefly:

Christ suffered to bring you to God, by being put to death in the flesh and being made alive in the spirit. (Salvation is not by cleansing of the flesh, but is by the resurrection of Christ.) Since Christ suffered in the flesh, you should follow his example, because your suffering in the flesh separates you from sin. Unbelievers will be surprised and will speak evil of you, but they will be judged. The reason for preaching the gospel, even to those who have died as a result of persecution, is so that while human standards judge a person while in the flesh, that person can live by God's standards.

4:7-11. What does Peter have in mind when he writes that "the end (*telos*) of all things is near"? Some have seen a reference to the impending destruction of Jerusalem, but there is no internal evidence to link Peter's words with that event. The more likely option is that Peter was anticipating the return of Jesus (cf. 2 Peter 3). The early church expected the imminent return of Jesus, and Peter in his second letter addresses the concern of some that the return has been delayed. In view of "the end," be sober-minded (*sophroneo*) and watchful (*nepho*) unto prayer. This verse begins a section of Scripture that emphasizes how to live "according to God" (4:6). The two imperatives of v. 7 emphasize the need to be alert unto (*eis*) prayer. This means that one should cultivate these characteristics for the purpose of effective prayer. One of the greatest enemies of prayer in the Christian life is lack of alertness. Prayer is difficult when one is mentally tired, when one cannot see the needs or the challenges, and when one is distracted. Prayer is a part of living "in the spirit."

4:8-9. In these verses, several participles function as imperatives, in dependent clauses constructed around the two verbs in v. 7. As a first priority, "having intense (fervent) love for one another (cf. 1:22), because love covers a large number of sins." The final phrase of v. 8 is quoted from Prov. 10:12. "Being hospitable to one another without complaining (murmuring)." Hospitality may be related to the fact the recipients of the letter were traveling and living in a foreign land.

How to Live According to God's Will
4:6   Live according to God…
    4:7   Be sober-minded and be watchful in order to pray
    4:8   Having intense love for one another
    4:9   Being hospitable to one another without grumbling
    4:10   Serving as good stewards of God's variegated grace

---

4:10-11. "As each one received a gift, serving (*diakoneo*) one another as good stewards of the variegated grace of God." This sentence relates to the "one another" instructions of vv. 8-9. God's grace gives different gifts to each Christian. Gift (*charisma*) is related to grace (*charis*). God gives gifts; Christ gives gifts (Eph. 4), and the Spirit gives gifts (1 Cor. 12). The gifts God gives are for serving others. Every Christian is called to serve others. Steward (*oikonomos*) is usually a description of household managers. The two "if clauses" are first class conditions, reflecting reality. A good translation can use the word "when." "When someone speaks, as an utterance of God; when someone serves, with strength which God supplies." The result is that God is glorified in everything through Jesus Christ. The doxological description of Jesus is brief and is concluded by an "amen" (so be it).

4:12-19. The term of address, "Beloved," is repeated from 2:11. "Do not be surprised (cf. 4:4) at the fire (*purosis*, literally, the burning) among you which comes to you as a trial, as something strange happening to you; but to the degree you share the sufferings of Christ, rejoice." The verb "rejoice" is a present imperative, often indicating continuing action, thus, "keep on rejoicing." The recipients were experiencing trials. Trials (*peirasmos*, 1:6) can serve as tests of faith. The word for testing in 1:7 (*dokimazo*) is not used here. Therefore, I have translated "comes to you as a trial" instead of "comes to you for your testing." The result of sharing the sufferings of Christ is rejoicing with exceeding joy when his glory is revealed. "That you might rejoice being exceedingly joyful."

4:14-16. Verses 14-18 contain several first class conditional sentences, reflecting real situations. "When you are insulted for the name of Christ, you are blessed (*makarios*, Matt. 5), because the Spirit of glory and of God rests on you." The reference is to the Holy Spirit. The presence of God is promised to Christians when they suffer and are insulted. Suffering and insults are certain. "But make sure that no one is suffering as a murderer, thief, criminal, or busybody. But when suffering is as a Christian, let him not be ashamed but let him glorify God in this name."

In 4:16 is one of only three occurrences of the word "Christian" in the New Testament. The more common word to describe followers of Jesus was "disciples," and that word appears more frequently in the New Testament. However, by the middle of the first century, Christian was a common designation of believers, often used in derision.

4:17. The time has come for judgment to begin at the house of God. Why the time for judgment has arrived is not stated in the text. The reference may be to the end of all things (4:7). The house of God (2:5, spiritual house) refers to the church. Some translations use "household" which also communicates accurately. The first class condition that follows can be translated "since," reflecting reality. "Since judgment begins with us, what will be the end of the ones disobeying the gospel of God?"

4:18-19. "If a righteous one is barely saved (a true statement), where will the ungodly and sinners appear?" This alludes to Proverbs 11:31 LXX. "Therefore, the ones suffering according to the will of God, to a faithful Creator let them entrust (*paratithemi,* to deposit for protection or safekeeping) their souls in doing good." *Paratithemi* is a present imperative, suggesting the need to continually commit our souls to God. "Doing good" is a theme in 1 Peter (2:14, 15, 20; 3:6, 17; 4:19). Doing good is always a right option, even in times of suffering and insult.

1 Peter 5

[Note: it is suggested that the student read the introductory materials in this guide before beginning any individual preparatory reading and analysis.]

CONTENT

The outline and paragraphing included in the Content section of each chapter are only suggestions or guides. The student is encouraged to identify the paragraphs and subsections within each paragraph to assist in his or her own study. In modern translations, there is general agreement about how to divide this chapter into paragraphs.

Outline of the Chapter
5:1-4 Instructions to church leaders
Note: v. 5 is sometimes included with 5:1-4 in paragraphing
5:5-11 Instructions and encouragement for Christians
5:12-14 Wisdom with faith helps us pray with confidence

Overview of the Chapter

The "therefore" of 5:1 connects the admonitions of this chapter with what has gone before. The chapter seems to function both as a closing to the third section of the book (3:13-5:11), and as a closing for the entire book. The theme of the third section of the book is suffering. In 5:1-11 are instructions about proper attitudes and conduct in the face of sufferings.

The plot of the book of 1 Peter can be described in this way: God's intention to bless his people (1:1-2:10), how to live in this world (2:11-3:12), even in the face of suffering (3:13-5:14).

In Chapter 5, continuing the use of terms of address, instructions are given to church leaders (5:1-4) and younger men (5:5). The section in 5:6-11 seems to include all of the recipients of the letter.

The last three verses serve as the closing salutation.

STUDY HELPS

5:1-5. "Therefore" connects this paragraph with what has gone before, as does the reference to the sufferings of Christ. The exhortation of vv. 1-4 is specifically directed to the elders (*presbuteros*). The context indicates that this group of church leaders also served as shepherds in that they shepherd (*poimaino*) the flock of God, and they are responsible as overseers, exercising oversight (*episkopeo*, the verb form of *episkopos*, overseer). With one exception, New Testament references to church leaders as elders, shepherds (pastors), and overseers (bishops) use plural nouns, referring to a group of leaders. In the only singular use in the New Testament, in reference to church leaders, Peter identifies himself also as an elder, mostly likely meaning in the context that he also served as an elder-shepherd-overseer. Peter writes to the elders as a fellow-elder, not as an apostle. Peter also identifies himself as a witness of Christ's sufferings and one who shares the glory to be revealed. Peter was an eyewitness of Jesus' life. "Suffering" likely refers to the crucifixion. To share in "the glory to be revealed" anticipates the return of Jesus.

5:2-3. The command to shepherd the flock is aorist imperative. Jesus used this verb in his conversation with Peter in John 21. The descriptive nouns—elders, overseers, and shepherds or pastors—were used interchangeably in the first century (Acts 20:17, 28; Tit. 1:5, 7), indicating that in each local congregation there was only one group of leaders. They were sometimes called elders, sometimes called overseers, and sometimes called shepherds or pastors. Good shepherds are among the flock so that the flock is among the shepherds. Some Greek manuscripts omit the verbal participle (*episkopeo*). Perhaps the omission occurred because of hesitancy to intermingle the distinct church offices that came to be identified. The task of oversight was to be assumed not of coercion, but voluntarily according to God, not for monetary gain but willingly. The instructions continue in 5:3, "not as lording over the inheritance but being examples for the flock."

5:4. "When the Chief Shepherd appears, you will receive the unfading crown of glory." Peter refers to Jesus as Shepherd (2:25) and now as Chief Shepherd (cf. Heb. 13:20, great Shepherd). The appearance of the Chief Shepherd refers to Jesus' return. Receiving a crown is a common metaphor (2 Tim. 4:8; James 1:12; Rev. 2:10, 3:11).

5:5. The younger men are addressed in the context of the instructions to the elders. "Likewise, younger men are to be subject to the elders." The term "elders" is sometimes used in the Bible simply to refer to older men, but here it seems that the context demands a reference to the church leaders described in vv. 1-4.

"All of you" could refer to the two groups that have already been mentioned in Chapter 5, or it could refer to all of the members of the church. There is no reason to limit the reference, especially in light of the "one another" reference and since the instructions continue in vv. 6-11, seemingly referring to all Christians. "All of you clothe yourselves (*egkomboomai*, gird) with humility toward one another." Humility is an attitude that is most easily seen in the context of relationships. The reason for "wearing" humility is because God gives grace (favor) to the humble but opposes the proud. The phrase is a quotation from Prov. 3:34 LXX.

5:6-11. Literally, the text reads, "Therefore, humble yourselves under God's mighty hand, so that he will exalt you in time (at the proper season), all your cares casting on him, because to him it matters concerning you." The last phrase is usually translated, "he cares for you." To readers who were undergoing persecution and felt pushed down more than lifted up, this message mattered. God is the one who takes care of exalting us. Our job is to be humble.

5:7. The dependent participle phrase, "casting your cares," points back to the main verb, humble yourselves.

5:8. Be sober (*nepho*) and be watchful (*gregoreuo*, be alert) are imperatives. See 1:13 and 4:7 for similar instructions. One's thinking, how and what one thinks, is a first line of defense against temptation and anxieties and is essential in maintaining a vibrant prayer life. This verse speaks about temptation. Why should one be sober-minded and alert? "Because your adversary lives (*peripateo*, literally walks) as a roaring lion, seeking someone to devour." The verb "to walk" is a metaphor for "to live" in many New Testament contexts. The adversary continually lives as a roaring lion; there is never a time when the adversary is not thinking about devouring someone. The emphasis is more on continuity and strong opposition than on stealth. Satan's purpose is always the same—destroy and kill.

5:9. The good news is that the efforts of the adversary can be resisted. In the phrase, "Resist (stand against) him, strong (*stereos*) in faith," the verb "resist" is an imperative (Jas. 4:7). Important to the resistance of a Christian is the knowledge that the same kind of suffering is being undergone (*epiteleo*) by your brothers in the world." The passive verb means the sufferings are being experienced or fulfilled by someone else. The text does not make clear whether the sufferings "are being undergone by the brothers" or "are being completed in the brothers." The conclusion is the same. Others are experiencing persecution; being persecuted was not uncommon for Christians in Peter's day.

5:10-11. "After a little time of suffering, may the God of all grace who himself called you to his eternal glory in Christ restore, confirm, strengthen, and establish you." The third person optative verb forms are translated as wishes rather than future certainties, "may he do these things for you," even though the all-powerful God who cares for you will certainly do these things. The short doxology at 5:11 is similar to the one at 4:11.

5:12-14. The conclusion of the letter, as was common in the Greek letter form, sends greetings and provides details about Silas who served as Peter's secretary or scribe (amanuensis), as the one who carried the letter, or both. "Through Silas…I have written to you briefly." Peter briefly summarizes the contents of the letter: "exhorting and testifying that this is the true grace of God." Peter often mentions grace in this letter (1:10, 13; 2:3; 3:7; 4:10; 5:5, 10, 12). "In which you stand firm" is an imperative: "in which you are to stand firm."

5:13. The phrase, "she who is in Babylon," likely refers to a church rather than to a specific Christian woman who was known so well that she did not have to be named. Babylon almost certainly refers to Rome (see Introduction). Mark is John Mark, whom we know from his travels with Paul and Barnabas on the first missionary journey (Acts 13). Although John Mark returned home (to Jerusalem, cf. Acts 12:12), Barnabas wanted to take him on the second missionary journey (Acts 15:36-41). Later in his ministry, Paul valued the work of John Mark (Col. 4:10; 2 Tim. 4:11). A close relationship between Peter and Mark apparently developed. Eusebius writes of the relationship, referring to the writings of Papias. In this verse, Peter refers to Mark as his son, not in a physical sense but in a spiritual sense. Peter may have had a part in the conversion of Mark to Christianity, but the use of the description "son" may mean only that Peter served as a father figure and mentor to Mark.

5:14. "Greet one another with a kiss of love." The kiss was a customary greeting among family members and very close friends, as it is still today in some cultures. In Rom. 16:16, there is a reference to a "holy kiss." Peter's closing desire is for peace to all of you (plural) who are in Christ. This reflects the Jewish greeting "Shalom," used both on arriving and on departing. Even in times of persecution, those who are "in Christ" can know peace.

As mentioned in the Introduction, the absence of personal greetings is sometimes explained by the suggestion that 1 Peter was a circular letters.

Introduction to Second Peter

For many Christians, the little book of 2 Peter is among the least known of all of the books of the New Testament. As one of the General Letters, it does not have many internal indications of its historical context so its study is not easily connected to the study of other sections of the New Testament. No specific groups of people or places can be identified.

For many Bible students, awareness of 2 Peter is limited to a few favorite passages. Some texts that readily come to mind are 1:5-7 with the list of Christian virtues, 1:20-21 concerning the inspiration of Scripture, 2:20-22 about the danger of leaving Christianity, and 3:8-13 about the end of the world. The admonition to "grow in grace and knowledge" (3:18) is also well-known and often cited.

The book of 2 Peter is theologically rich and provides wise counsel for life. Now is a good time to do a little digging in your own Bible and unpack the beauty of this little book.

Authorship

The authorship of 2 Peter has been much disputed with many questions having been raised about the traditional view that it was written by Peter. The authorship questions have to do with internal concerns such as style and content, and external concerns, primarily the hesitancy of the early church to accept the book as canonical. The delay in the acceptance of the book as canonical was related to the question of authorship, not to the contents of the book. A brief introduction cannot deal with every detail of every question. The author of this Bible Study Guide accepts Peter's authorship, seeing no compelling evidence to the contrary. Regardless of one's view, the inspiration of the book as part of God's Word is not in question.

The book claims to be written by Symeon Peter (1:1). The Semitic spelling would be unusual in a pseudonymous book. The author is eyewitness of the transfiguration (1:16-18) and says he is writing a second letter (3:1). If Peter is not the author, we do not have the first letter. Nothing in the letter contradicts other biblical teachings. Stylistically, the letter is distinct from 1 Peter, but considering factors such as language, themes, occasion, and the use or not of a scribe, such is not a sufficient reason for rejecting Peter's authorship.

Acceptance into the New Testament Canon

External concerns about authorship primarily focus on the delayed acceptance of the letter by the early church. Eusebius (4th century AD) classified writings as accepted, disputed, and spurious. He accepted 1 Peter and put Hebrews, James, 2 Peter, 2 John, and 3 John in the disputed category. The Marcionite canon (AD 154) does not include 2 Peter, but Marcion rejected many other New Testament books. The Muratorian Fragment (c. AD 180) does not include 2 Peter, but the fragment is damaged and also fails to include Hebrews, James, and 1 Peter. Chrysostom and Theodore of Mopsuestia (late 4th century AD) rejected all of the General Letters. The book of 2 Peter is included in p^{72} in the third or fourth century (the early papyrus copies of the biblical text are numbered). In the first two centuries, 2 Peter is quoted or alluded to by Clement of Rome (AD 95), Justin Martyr (AD 115-165), and Irenaeus (AD 130-200). In summary, while the canonicity of the letter was questioned, good evidence exists in the early centuries for its inclusion.

Date and Place of Writing, Recipients

To accept Peter's authorship places the date of writing early, before the death of Peter in the 60s. Rejecting Peter's authorship opens the way for conjectures concerning a later date. W.F. Albright noted similarities between 2 Peter and the Dead Sea Scrolls and suggested an early date. The letter can be dated in the early to mid-60s, shortly after the first letter. Peter may be anticipating his impending death (1:14-15). Nothing is said in the letter to help us determine the place of writing. If 2 Peter 3:1 refers to the book of 1 Peter, one can assume the same recipients.

Genre of the Book

What kind of literature is 2 Peter? It resembles a first century letter written in the Greek epistolary form since it has a typical opening salutation and closing section. The lack of personal greetings may indicate that it was a letter intended for Christians in various locations (cf. Galatians, Ephesians, James, 1 Peter, and 1 John).

Purpose of the Book, Themes in the Book
    A primary theme of 2 Peter is false teaching. False teachers and false teaching are treated in the second chapter; the third chapter deals with the perception of a delayed return of Jesus. The book describes Christ in a number of ways. The Christian life depends on knowledge for growth and maturity that seeks holiness and godliness. The book also has a focus on last things. Themes that run as threads throughout the book include salvation, Scripture, knowledge, remembering, false teaching, and the return of the Lord.

Brief Outline of 1 Peter
1:1-2, Salutation
1:3-21, true knowledge of Christ
2:1-22, false teachers
3:1-18, return of Christ, closing exhortations

Resources
See Introduction to 1 Peter.

2 Peter 1

[Note: it is suggested that the student read the introductory materials in this guide before beginning any individual preparatory reading and analysis.]

CONTENT

The outline and paragraphing included in the Content section are suggestions or guides. The student should identify the paragraphs and subsections within each paragraph as part of his or her own reading and study. The division of the biblical text into paragraphs is fairly standard in modern translations.

Outline of the Chapter
1:1-2	Salutation and greetings
1:3-11	The Christian's calling and election demand faithful growth
1:12-15	Peter's impending death
1:16-18	Eyewitnesses of Christ's glory
1:19-21	The trustworthy prophetic word

Overview of the Chapter

     This chapter begins with one long sentence. The customary salutation is followed by several descriptive sections related to the "equally valuable faith." Those to whom Peter writes are described as those who obtained a faith equally valuable with us. This faith has several dimensions—God's calling and gifts; the believer's response; the results of such faith; the assurance of such faith.

     After a brief description of his personal circumstances, Peter returns to the primary theme of the chapter—the true knowledge of Jesus Christ. He sets forth the foundations for faith, based on the word of God.

STUDY HELPS

1:1-2. Simon Peter is identified as slave (*doulos*) and apostle of Jesus Christ. "Slave" reflects his submission. "Apostle" asserts both his authority and his status as an eyewitness (Acts 1). For more on Peter's authorship, see the Introduction.

The extended introduction to the book (1:1-11) is theologically rich. The recipients of the letter are those who have obtained (*lagchano*) equally precious faith. The verb *lagchano* relates to casting lots, thus, to determine by lot (Acts 1:17). The verb is usually translated "to obtain" or "to receive." They have arrived at faith through God's gifting, calling, and choosing (1:3-10). The ambiguity of the verb is reflected in vv. 3-7. God's desired result comes when God's actions and human response meet. The faith of the believer is grounded in God's faithfulness. The recipients have arrived at a faith which is "equally valuable" (*isotimos*). This faith is received by the righteousness of Jesus Christ, who is described as God and Savior. Biblically, the righteousness of a believer is grounded in Christ's righteousness, but one who reads Peter's letters through the eyes of Paul's teachings about the declared legal righteousness available to a Christian through Christ will easily miss the importance of the concept for Peter. Peter uses the word to describe a way of life that is characterized by holiness, ethical dealings, and fairness. The description of Christ as "God and Savior" is a clear affirmation of Christ's deity. Some studies see in the phrase a reference to God as Father and Jesus Christ as Savior (see also comments on 1:2).

1:2. "Grace and peace be multiplied" is much like 1 Pet. 1:2. Grace and peace are given to the believer "in the knowledge of God and of Jesus our Lord." Knowledge (*epignosis*) is not merely mental; it is an experiential, personal knowledge, the ability to recognize and discern. Knowledge is a theme of 2 Peter. The basic noun that is translated as knowledge, *gnosis*, is used in 1:5-6, while the related verb, *ginosko*, is used in 1:20 and 3:3. The Greek word, *epignosis*, is used in 1:2, 3, 8; 2:20, while the related verb *epignosko* is used twice in 2:21. Another word, *gnorizo*, to make known, is used in 1:16. The nuances of these words are difficult to reflect in English translation. An easy way to make the distinction is to translate *gnosis* as knowledge and *epignosis* as full knowledge. False teaching is often the result of impartial knowledge (see additional comments in Chapter 2). The ambiguity of v. 1, whether the reference is both to God the Father and Jesus Christ, occurs again in v. 2, "the knowledge of God and Jesus our Lord." The question is not easily resolved, but fortunately the meaning and message of 2 Peter are little impacted by the ambiguity.

1:3-11. The text of 1:3-7 is one long sentence in Greek. The transition is smooth from the salutation to 1:3 with the word *hos* (so, thus, not translated in many translations). The truths presented in 1:1-2 are connected to 1:3-4. "His divine power (*dunamis*)" refers back to vv. 1-2, either to God the Father or to Jesus Christ. That power has granted us everything related to life and godliness, through the true knowledge (*epignosis*) of the one calling us by his glory and virtue (*arete*, excellence, 1 Pet. 2:10). Peter's focus on knowledge should be understood in the context of the false teachers he is combatting (see Chapter 2). In this context, the translation of *epignosis* as "true knowledge" helps make clear the contrast.

1:4. "By which things he has given us precious and very great (*megistos*) promises so that by them you may become sharers (*koinonos*) of divine nature, having escaped the corruption in the world because of evil desires." The divine (*theios*) nature is a nature that is godly or god-like.

1:5-7. "For this same reason" refers to what has gone before, probably to the phrase, "in order to become sharers...." One becomes a participant in the divine nature as described in vv. 5-7. Several items are included in the list. The items are straightforward and easily understood.

"All diligence giving (*pareisphero*, literally, to bring alongside, aorist participle), fully supply (*epichoregeo*) in your faith virtue (*arete*, excellence, 1:3)." Faith is not just mental acceptance of the truth; faith involves acting on the truth. In some biblical contexts, the word "faith" is best translated as faithfulness. *Arete* is sometimes translated as "moral excellence."

"And in virtue, knowledge (*gnosis*)." The use of *gnosis* instead of *epignosis* illustrates that the two words were at times used somewhat interchangeably. One might expect in the context of 2 Peter the use of the more intense form (*epignosis*). Some have observed that *gnosis* is the first step toward *epignosis*, as we sometimes say that knowledge precedes wisdom.

"And in knowledge, self-control (*egkrateia*)." This noun appears in only two other New Testament contexts (Acts 24:25; Gal. 5:23).

"And in self-control, perseverance (*hupomone*)." This word is sometimes translated as endurance or patience.

"And in perseverance, godliness." Several words are translated as "godliness" in the New Testament. Here the word is *eusebeia* (holiness, piety) a word that Paul uses frequently in the Pastoral Letters (1 Tim. 2:2; 3:16; 4:7, 8; 6:3, 5, 6, 11).

"And in godliness, brotherly love (*philadelphia*)."

"And in brotherly love, love." Love is the capstone of the list. The list should not be thought of as sequential, so that each additional quality cannot be added until the previous one is mastered. Nor should the list be thought of as complete or all-inclusive. Cultivating these qualities in one's life makes one more like God.

1:8-11. The conditional participle introduces a conditional sentence that functions much like a first class condition. To reflect the reality of the condition, I prefer to translate with the word "when." The negative with negative characteristics (not useless or unproductive) may sound strange to the English-speaking ear. "When these qualities are present and abundant, they make you not [to be] useless or unproductive in the knowledge (*epignosis*) of our Lord Jesus Christ." The preposition *eis* suggests that the Christian is moving toward this knowledge.

1:9. The one in whom these things are not present is blind, being short-sighted (near-sighted, "of dim vision" may fit the context best), being forgetful (literally, forgetfulness receiving or having, *lambano*) of the cleansing from his past sins. The motivation for sharing the divine nature and escaping worldly desires is the knowledge of God and his promises for life and godliness, that is, awareness of our forgiveness. One without such knowledge is easily lured back to the world.

1:10-11. Therefore, be more diligent to make your calling and election sure (*bebaios*, with a stable base). Christians are called and selected by God. They can respond to God in such a way as to secure their calling and selection. Doing these things, you will not stumble at any time. The double negative is often translated "by no means." In this way, an entrance will be richly supplied (*epichorogeo*, 1:5) to you into the eternal kingdom of our Lord and Savior Jesus Christ.

1:12-15. Peter writes in this paragraph of his impending death. Peter will be ready always to remind them of these things (see 3:1-2), although they know and are established in them in the existing truth (*parouse* is the word translated "existing," related to *parousia*, thus, the present truth, the truth they have). "I consider it right, as long as I am in this body (literally, tabernacle, earthly dwelling, cf. 2 Cor. 5), to stir you up as a reminder, knowing that the laying aside (*apotheosis*) of my earthly dwelling is soon, as our Lord Jesus Christ has showed me. I will also be diligent so that after my departure (*exodos*), you will be able to remember these things at all times."

Seeking to Know Christ Fully
- Christians intentionally add certain characteristics to their lives
- Christians incorporate these qualities into their lives and commit to growth
- Christians maintain these qualities because they remember their salvation
- Christians live intentionally in response to their calling and selection by God

---

1:16-18. Peter supports what he is saying about full knowledge by sharing his experience as an eyewitness. The main verb of the sentence is "to make known" (*gnorizo*). It is preceded by an aorist participle whose action precedes the main verb, and a present participle whose action is contemporary with or follows the main verb. "We made known to you the power and presence (*parousia*, presence, or coming) of our Lord Jesus Christ, not by having followed cleverly devised myths but by being eyewitnesses of his greatness." The phrase, "cleverly devised myths," likely refers to the teachings of the false teachers. Peter was an eyewitness of Jesus' majesty at the Transfiguration. The context of Peter's description is made clear in the next verses. This eyewitness description of the Transfiguration is consistent with Peter's authorship.

1:17-18. Peter says that Jesus, at the Transfiguration (see Matt. 17:5 and parallels), received honor and glory from God, based on the words that were spoken: "this is my beloved Son with whom I am well-pleased." This phrase is a Messianic title (Ps. 2:7) and is stated also at Jesus' baptism (Matt. 3:17). Peter and those who were with him personally heard the words when they were with Jesus in the Mount of Transfiguration.

1:19-21. "We have the more certain prophetic word, you do well to pay attention to it as a light shining in a dark place until the day dawns and the light bearer rises up in your hearts." The prophetic word could refer to Old Testament prophecy, the truth of the apostles (1:12), or the word from heaven that confirmed Jesus' identity. Since the voice from heaven was citing Old Testament Scripture, my preference is a reference to the Old Testament. "Made more certain" is a comparative form of *bebaios*. The Old Testament was being confirmed by the events of Jesus' life. The prophetic word is as a light that shines in darkness. The Old Testament shone in the darkness of ignorance until the coming of Jesus. Light bearer is a literal translation of *phosphoros*; it is also translated as morning star or day star. Here is obviously refers to Jesus (Rev. 2:28; 22:16) and not to Satan or some other person. The dawning of a day is marked by the coming of light. The light bearer is described as rising up in human hearts. By understanding a reference to the Old Testament and an application to Jesus Christ, the reading of the passage is clear. The dawning of day and the light bearer arising in human hearts does not have to be future for Peter's readers. It was future in the context described in the verse, when the light was shining in the darkness, but is a reality when Peter writes.

1:20-21. "Know (the verb is a participle but is translated as an imperative based on the context) first of all that all prophecy of Scripture is not of one's own explanation (*epilusis*, application, interpretation). No prophecy of the past was brought forth by human will, but carried along by the Holy Spirit men spoke from God."

Scripture is from God, given to fulfill God's purpose in the world (2 Tim. 3:16-17). God guided the writing and delivery of his word. The reference is clearly to Old Testament Scripture (as is also the case in 2 Tim. 3:16). These verses anticipate the instructions about false teachers that will begin in 2:1. Remember that there were no chapter divisions in the original manuscripts. God's word is sure, understandable, from God, and given through human beings who were guided by the Holy Spirit.

2 Peter 2

Note: it is suggested that the student read the introductory materials in this guide before beginning any individual preparatory reading and analysis.]

CONTENT
The outline and paragraphing included in the Content section of each chapter are intended as suggestions or guides. The student should identify the paragraphs and subsections within each paragraph to assist with her or his own understanding. Consulting your Bible may be helpful. The division of the biblical text into paragraphs is fairly standard in modern translations.

Outline of the Chapter
2:1-10a   The presence of false teachers
    2:1-3   Introduction of the false teachers
    2:4-10a   The punishment and doom of the false teachers
2:10b-22   The attitudes, conduct, nature, and influence of the false teachers described
    2:10b-14   Depravity of the false teachers
    2:15-22   Deceptions of the false teachers

Overview of the Chapter
    Some parts of this chapter parallel verses in the book of Jude. There seems to be literary borrowing, but who borrowed from whom is not clear. Probably, Jude referred to Peter's prophecy since Jude wrote after Peter's death. The possibility that both authors borrowed from a common source has also been suggested.

    Internal evidence concerning the identity of the false teachers is minimal. Some of the false teachers may have been Christians who, after becoming believers, returned to the world (2:13, 15, 19-20), although the reference in vv. 19-20 could also be to those influenced by the false teachers.

In a quick overview of the chapter, one can note that the false teachers were heretical, denied the Master, had an immoral lifestyle, caused Christianity to be slandered, were greedy, were deceivers, despised authority, found pleasure in carousing, were sharing in the Christian love feasts, were adulterous, were sinners, influenced others to sin, and were enslaved to immorality.

STUDY HELPS

2:1-3. Peter speaks of the future presence (future tense of *eimi*, to be) of false teachers among his readers, just as God's people have always experienced the presence of false prophets. Based on the specific details set forth in the text, Peter is describing the actual presence of false teachers, not the characteristics of past false prophets. Some of the wording seems to anticipate future events, perhaps the logical result of what is already occurring.

"They will sneak in (bring in secretly) destructive heresies...." Here, heresies are false teachings. Such teachings often hide error by combining it with truth. "...even denying the Master who redeemed (*agorazo*, to purchase, as in the marketplace) them, bringing upon themselves swift destruction." "Master" is *despotes* (lord) and was sometimes used of slaveowners. Here it seems to refer to the Lord Jesus. Some think the false teachers were denying Jesus' deity in parallel to those described in 1 John. In this context, a preferable understanding is that they were denying Jesus' lordship (2:10). There is a word play in the two phrases: they bring in **destructive** heresies, and they are themselves are **destroyed**. That they had been redeemed suggests that they had formerly been Christians but had subsequently fallen away from the faith. Their "destruction" may refer to the destruction of their faith or to eternal destruction.

2:2. Many will follow their immorality (*aselgeia*, licentiousness, sensuality), with the result that the way of truth will be blasphemed. That the way of truth was maligned because of the false teachers may suggest again that they were formerly Christians and that they were still identified with the Christian believers. Nonbelievers watch the actions of those who profess faith.

2:3. "In their greed they will exploit you (*emporeuomai*, compare our word emporium) with false (*plastos*, carefully formed, compare our word plastic) words." Greed may be seen in financial pursuits or in seeking after position and prestige. The false teachers were seeking followers. "...of whom the judgment long overdue does not linger (*argeo*, delay) and their destruction does not slumber (*nustazo*, figuratively, delay)." All will receive from the Lord that which is due them in his good time.

2:4-10a. After giving a brief description of the false teachers, Peter speaks of their impending punishment and doom. This section builds on and expands the mention of judgment and destruction in v. 3. Peter uses several historical examples to show that God's judgment is certain. God did not spare the angels that sinned; he did not spare the ancient world in the day of Noah; and he condemned the cities of Sodom and Gomorrah. In the same paragraph, Peter shows that God delivers the righteous. Analyzing the construction of the passage, "if...then" has four conditions (v. 4, 5, 6, 7-8) before it reaches the conclusion in v. 9. The conditions are reality and can be translated "since."

"If God did not spare the angels who sinned...." The conditional construction appears only in v. 4 but seems to extend through all of the examples given, as reflected in a majority of translations. See Jude 6 for a parallel reference to angels who sinned. God did not spare them but in chains (or pits) of darkness he imprisoned [them] in hell (*tartaroo*, a word that means hell, Tartarus, is here made into a verb), kept (*tereo*) for judgment. A textual variant that alters only one letter of the reading is the cause of the translation variation between chains and pits. The verb, *tartaroo*, appears only here in the New Testament. The point is that God judged the sinning angels.

"And did not spare the ancient world, but preserved Noah...." When he brought a flood on the ungodly world, God judged the world of Noah's day, but protected Noah who was a preacher of righteousness.

"And he condemned the cities...." God condemned Sodom and Gomorrah (Gen. 19:24-28) by incinerating them, setting forth a clear example for those who would be ungodly afterward.

"And he rescued righteous Lot...." Lot is described as oppressed or worn down by the sensual (*aselgeia,* immoral) conduct of the wicked. Verse 8 repeats and expands slightly the last phrase of v. 7. By what Lot saw and heard, being among them day after day, his righteous soul was tormented by their lawless actions.

2:9-10a. Here concludes the extended thought (vv. 4-10a). In v. 9 is the apodosis, the "then" statement. If God did all of the things in vv. 4-8, then God knows how to rescue the godly from temptation and to keep the unrighteous for punishment, especially those who follow the flesh in unclean lusts and despise authority. Who is Peter describing? Who are those who follow the flesh and despise authority? He is describing the false teachers.

They despise authority. Some think the reference to "authority" refers to angels, others connect it with church leaders. The statement is general enough to refer to all types of authority, but the preferable application in the context refers to the authority and lordship of Jesus Christ.

2:10b-14. The false teachers are presumptuous and arrogant. When insulting or blaspheming "glories" they do not tremble. The meaning of "glories" is difficult to understand. The plural form that is used can be literally translated as "glorious ones." In studies of this passage, the word has been connected with the angels (primarily on the basis of v. 11), with church leaders, and with the glories of Christ (see 1 Pet. 1:11 for a parallel text, see also 2 Pet. 1:16-18). If the authority despised in v. 10a is the authority of Christ, insulting the "glories" of Christ likely continues the same line of thought. Such would connect naturally with the idea of questioning Christ's authority.

2:11. "But even angels, being greater in strength and power, do not bring a slanderous judgment against them before the Lord." The purpose of this verse is to draw a contrast between the restraint in judgment of angelic beings and the arrogance and presumption of the false teachers. The false teachers were bold in their immorality, perhaps teaching others that such immoral activity was acceptable (see 2:18-19). They were generous with their criticisms, accusations, and judgments. The natural contrast in this verse is between good angelic beings (not the angels of v. 4) and the false teachers. Angels do not bring slanderous judgments, even against lesser beings such as the false teachers ("against them"). The false teachers reject Christ Jesus and his glories, or they reject his "glorious" disciples, or they reject other "glories," meaning glorious ones or glorious things that are not specifically identified in the verse. The application is the same. The false teachers stand condemned, kept for punishment at the day of judgment (v. 9). For an interesting parallel to v. 11, see Jude 9 where the archangel Michael refused to pronounce judgment against the devil.

2:12-14. These verses describe the depth of the depravity of the false teachers. Verse 12 is much like Jude 10, continuing the parallel previously noted. While I have begun a new subsection in this verse, the connection to what has gone before is clear. This paragraph is a description of the false teachers in the context of fleshly desires, despising authority, and slandering glories. That the false teachers are irrational connects to the theme of knowledge. Because they are without reasoning, they are ignorant and without understanding. One who has access to knowledge and refuses to use it is no better than one who does not have access. In vv. 12-14, the false teachers are described in various ways, with a series of grammatical phrases that are piled one upon the other.

2:12. "These (the false teachers) are like unreasoning natural animals, having been born [naturally] for capture and corruption (*phthora*, destruction)." In some manuscripts the word "natural" is transposed. The choices are that (1) the false teachers are like unreasoning natural animals, born for capture..., or (2) they are they like unreasoning animals, born naturally for capture. The meaning of the second option is that they were born with an unreasoning nature that makes them suitable only for capture and destruction.

"In the things of which they are ignorant, they are blaspheming. In their corruption (*phthora*), they will be corrupted (*kataphtheiro*)." They talk about things they do not know and understand. The repetition of the idea of corruption is noteworthy.

2:13-14. "...suffering wrong as the wages of doing wrong, counting as pleasure the day of indulgence (*truphe*, alternate reading, luxury)." The first phrase is unusual; perhaps it is a play on words. They suffer wrong *(adikeo)* as the wages of doing wrong *(adikia)*. The meaning in the second phrase depends on the definition of *truphe*. The verb can mean "to make the body weak through indulgence." The noun form can be translated as soft, delicate, effeminate, luxury or luxurious living. Because luxurious living was associated with banquets and orgies, the word sometimes comes into English as riotous living (KJV). The false teachers are being weakened and are perishing as a result of their luxury and indulgence. Because they are unable to see the final results, they count such actions as pleasure. The meaning is that they do not realize that the indulgence (luxurious days) they consider pleasure is wrong-doing for which they will one day suffer.

"...[S]pots *(spilos)* and blemishes *(momos*, blots) indulging in their deceits while they feast *(suneuocheo)* with you." *Spilos* is sometimes used to refer to unseen dangers as well as to stains. (For an explanation of two Greek words which differ by only one letter, see comments on Jude 11-13.) A key to understanding the verse is the recognition that the verb, *entruphao*, is a repetition of the idea couched in the noun *truphe*. To translate "indulgence" in both cases maintains the continuity that was clear in the original Greek text. The indulgence in deceitful luxuries occurs in the context of feasts with the Christians who are receiving Peter's letter. To what feasts does Peter refer? The reference could be to love feasts, but I prefer to render the verse more literally and say in translation only what the original text says. The parallel passage in Jude 13 uses a different word and clearly describes love feasts.

2:14. "...[H]aving eyes full of an adulteress and unceasing from sin, alluring unstable souls, having a heart exercised in covetousness, cursed children." The descriptive phrases are strung together with a minimum of conjunctions. Eyes full of an adulteress is usually translated as eyes full of adultery. With the previous mention of unclean desires (v. 10), there is no reason to interpret this as spiritual adultery. The false teachers were immoral. They enticed unstable persons (see vv. 18-19). They were training *(gumnazo*, our word gym) their hearts in covetousness. The idiom in the last phrase says they are under God's curse, literally, "children of cursing." The description as "children" should not be overemphasized. The point is that they participate in the works and words of their father, and that the result is cursing, the opposite of blessing.

2:15-22. The occurrence of another main verb provides a logical place to begin a new paragraph.

2:15-16. "Forsaking the right way, they have gone astray (*planao*, our word planet), following the way of Balaam of Beor, who loved the wages of doing wrong (*adikia*, see v. 13), but he had reproof of his own transgression, a mute donkey speaking with the voice of a man restrained the madness of the prophet." The story of Balaam (see Num. 22-25) is also mentioned in Jude 11.

2:17. "These are waterless springs and mists driven by a storm, for whom the gloom of darkness has been kept." A generally parallel reading occurs in Jude 12. The phrasing in the second part of 2:17 reflects 2:4 (see also Jude 6, 13.)

2:18-19. By speaking high-sounding and empty words they entice with fleshly desires and immorality (*aselgeia*, 2:2) those who barely escaped from those who live in error (*plane*, v. 15). They entice these by promising them freedom, even though they themselves (the false teachers) are slaves of corruption (*phthora*, v. 12). The play on words should be noticed—promising freedom while being enslaved. That the false teachers are slaves is proved by the last part of v. 19: "by what a person is overcome (*hettao*), by that also he is enslaved." The question is always pertinent: What controls you?

2:20-22. The immediate reference here is to those who were being enticed in vv. 18-19, not to the false teachers, although the principles can be applied in every situation. The first class condition is considered true. Those who were enticed were believers. These three verses summarize the section dealing with false teachers.

"If after having escaped the contaminations of the world by the knowledge of the Lord and Savior Jesus Christ, and in these again being entangled they are overcome (*hettao*), to them the last state is worse than the first." The escape from the world was completed (aorist active participle). To put it in other words, they had been saved. The fact that escape from the world is possible through the knowledge (*epignosis*) of Jesus Christ reflects the importance of "knowledge" as a theme of the book.

2:21. Their last condition was worse because it would have been better for them never to have known the way of righteousness than, having known it, to turn back from the holy commandment handed down to them. Verses 20-21 make clear that after knowing Jesus Christ, being saved, and escaping the world, it is possible to return to one's previous unsaved situation.

2:22. The situation described in vv. 20-21 reminds Peter of a proverb. What has happened to them is according to a true proverb: a dog returns to its own vomit (Prov. 26:11) and a sow after washing to wallowing in the mud.

2 Peter 3

[Note: it is suggested that the student read the introductory materials in this guide before beginning any individual preparatory reading and analysis.]

CONTENT
The outline and paragraphing included in the Content section of each chapter are intended only as suggestions or guides. The student is always encouraged to identify the paragraphs and subsections to assist in her or his own study. You are encouraged to use your own Bible. The division of the biblical text into paragraphs is fairly standard in modern translations.

Outline of the Chapter
3:1-7   The promise of the Lord's coming
3:8-13   the Day of the Lord
3:14-18   Be steadfast, doxology and closing

Overview of the Chapter
   In this chapter Peter turns to the third major theme of the letter. Some were questioning the promise of the Lord's coming due to the delay in his return. That some, about 30 years after Jesus' death, were questioning whether he would in fact return as promised can serve as encouragement to sustain Christians today as we await the same promise almost 2000 years after his death.
   As reflected in the outline above, this chapter gives details concerning the Day of the Lord and the end of the world. The book concludes with typical admonitions and a closing doxology.

STUDY HELPS
3:1-7. Peter is writing a second letter not long after the first. The first letter referred to in this passage is probably 1 Peter. Peter writes that both letters are intended to provide a reminder to stir up their sincere (*eilekrines*, pure, without contamination) mind,

to remember the words (*rhema*) spoken before by the holy prophets and the command of the Lord and Savior through your apostles. "The words of the prophets" refers to the Old Testament. The commandment (holy commandment, 2:21) of Jesus refers to apostolic teaching. "Your apostles" is an unusual wording.

3:3. First of all understand this: in the last days scoffers will come with scoffing, going forth according to their own desires or lusts. This phrase, "first of all," was used to mark off main points and does not necessarily anticipate a second point. The concept of "last days" is used in the Bible in various ways. The phrase is used to refer to the coming judgment of God on Israel, the last days of Judaism, and the judgment of God at the end of the world. Peter uses the phrase, "in the last days," to refer to his own day. That some were questioning the return of the Lord was not strange. The coming of such scoffers had been predicted.

3:4. The scoffers ask, "Where is the promise of his coming?" commenting that since the death of the fathers everything has continued without interruption from the creation. In the context, they are asking about Jesus' return. "The fathers" likely refers to the Old Testament leaders. The suggestion that "fathers" is a reference to the early Christians who had already died is plausible but less likely. The use of this wording with reference to deceased Christians is not attested to elsewhere. If the scoffers are to be identified with the false teachers of Chapter 2, they were questioning Jesus' authority and his return to judge the world.

3:5-7. Such scoffers, with their questions and commentary, are failing to notice (deliberately ignoring) the power of God's word, that is, of God's promises. The verb means to forget something or to hide something.

They fail to notice that, by the word of God the heavens existed long ago and the earth was formed out of water and by water. God spoke the heavens and the earth into existence by his powerful word.

It was also by God's word ("by which") that the world afterward was destroyed, being deluged with water. The plural form, "by which," may refer to promises or words (note the plural in 3:1). The focus of this passage is on the power of God's word.

By the same word the present heavens and earth have been kept, for fire being kept for a day of judgment and destruction of ungodly men. While it is true that evil angels will be judged (2:4), this verse clearly refers to judgment on human beings.

3:8-13. "Dear friends" is repeated from v. 1. As the scoffers are letting the power of God's word escape their notice (v. 5), the recipients of the letter are to make certain that something does not escape their notice: "just one day with the Lord is as a thousand years, and a thousand years as a single day." This saying alludes to Ps. 90:4. The point is not to make literal calculations that substitute one quantity for the other, but that from the viewpoint of an eternal God time is not a factor. How would one know which equality to use as a substitute? Is it one for a thousand, or a thousand for one? Because God is eternal and not limited by time, God's promises are not limited by time. Questions concerning the delay in Jesus' coming also arose in the first century in the church in Thessalonica (2 Thess. 2:1-3).

3:9. The "problem" is not that God is tarrying with respect to his promise. The "problem" is God's patience and compassion for the lost. God is long-suffering. This explanation of the delay in Jesus' return is unique to Peter. God wants all to reach repentance; God wants none to perish. God's desire is for the salvation of all. The idea that God chooses some and rejects others is unbiblical. God wants all to be saved (1 Tim. 2:4).

3:10. In this verse, "the day of the Lord" refers to the final judgment at the end of the world. The end of the world will come suddenly and unexpectedly (1 Thess. 5:2). On that day, the heavens will disappear with a whirring sound, a sound of rapidly moving air. The elements, the basic building blocks of the world (*kosmos*), will be dissolved by being burned up. Elements (*stoicheia*) is sometimes translated as celestial bodies (TEV, ESV), but basic building blocks fits the context better. The sequence— heavens, elements of the world, earth—functions whether one reads elements as building blocks or as celestial bodies. Finally, the earth with all of the activities done on it will be manifested.

In v. 10 is one of the most difficult textual problems in the New Testament. Despite the numerous conjectures that have been put forth, the original text is difficult to identify and the correct translation uncertain. The reading that is best supported uses the verb "will be found or discovered." But what would that verb mean in the context of 2 Peter 3? Since the normal meaning of the verb is reflected in equivalents such as "to be disclosed, to be manifested, to be laid bare," the meaning of the text is that the works that humans have done on the earth will remain visible and open to God so they can be judged by God.

The heavens will disappear, but God's word will continue (1 Pet. 1:23). The created physical world is finite and temporal. The physical world is dissolvable—heavens, heavenly bodies, the world and its elements, the earth. What remains when all else is dissolved are the human activities.

3:11-12. All these things thus being dissolved, that is, everything but the record of human activities, what kind of people is it necessary to be, in holy conduct (*anastrophe*) and godliness (*eusebeia*), expecting and eagerly awaiting the coming of the day of God? Through which (in the original text, the word "which" clearly refers to the day of God) the heavens will be dissolved being burned up, and the elements being burned will melt. The "dissolving of the heavens" and the "melting of the elements" are repeated from v. 10. All that exists physically will be destroyed.

Some have considered these statements as figurative and apocalyptic, denying the destruction of the physical realm. The text has no hint that the physical realm will continue. The new heaven and the new earth (v. 13) are not physical but spiritual (1 Cor. 15:35-58). The realities described in these verses are not to be understood symbolically, even though the wording is similar to the language of apocalyptic literature.

3:13. According to his (God's) promise (3:4-7), and based on the dependability of his word, we are waiting for a new heaven and a new earth, in which righteousness dwells. (See comments on 1:1-2 for Peter's use of righteousness to describe a lifestyle. God will establish his people, those who share his character.)

3:14-18. "Beloved" is repeated. "Therefore" (because of what has just been said), since you are waiting for these things, be diligent to be found by him in peace, without spot or blemish (2:13, 1 Pet. 1:19). The focus is on the lifestyle and attitude of believers. Faith results in holiness and peace.

3:15. And "consider the longsuffering of our Lord as salvation." The longsuffering of our Lord relates to God's patience and the delay in Jesus' return. The patience of God is intended to result in the salvation of more people.

Apparently, Peter identifies what he has just written with some of the writings of Paul that were known to his readers. For example, Paul also wrote about God's patience and desire for the salvation of all (1 Tim. 2:4). Paul had written to the same recipients, according to the wisdom given him. Considering the location of the recipients, a good guess regarding the writings Peter refers to is the book of Galatians. Considering the theme of the coming of Jesus, the letters to the Thessalonians could fit the description.

3:16. The meaning of the text is that Peter knows the things he is writing are difficult to grasp. This understanding provides the connection to what he writes in this verse: "in all of his letters where Paul spoke of these things, there are some things hard to understand." A more literal reading says, "as also in all of his letters speaking in them of these things, in which are things hard to understand." Which things? Several of the themes treated in 2 Peter are difficult; Paul's writings about the same themes were also hard to understand. "...[T]hings which the untaught and unstable twist (*stebloo*, pervert, distort), as the rest of the Scriptures, to their own destruction." Scriptures generally refers to the Old Testament, but here either the written teachings about the themes are being distorted or the writings of Paul are being distorted. If the latter, Paul's writings are being placed on an equal plane with the Old Testament writings.

3:17. "Beloved" is again included as a term of address. "You then, knowing these things ahead of time, be on guard." What did they know in advance? The phrase likely refers to the teachings in Chapter 3, but the verse could also serve as a summary of the entire book. The reason to be on guard is stated: "lest they, being carried away by the error (*plane*) of wicked men, fall from their own stability (*sterigmos*, firmness, steadfastness).

3:18. The final admonition of the book serves as a contrast to falling away from a firm faith. How can one remain firm in faith? The antidote is this: "grow in the grace and knowledge of our Lord and Savior." The imperative calls attention to the necessity of continually developing knowledge, reflecting again that knowledge is a primary theme in the book. The best guard against error is knowledge. (See Jude 20 for a parallel text.)

The book closes with a doxology. "To him be glory both now and on that eternal day." The absence of personal greetings and other components of the typical extended closing may suggest that the letter was intended for Christians in various churches and that it was circulated as a circular letter.

Introduction to First John

The three shortest books penned by John, especially 2 John and 3 John, are often all but ignored in Bible classes. For example, in collegiate Bible classes, the shorter writings of John are sometimes included in a study of the Johannine corpus—all of the writings of John. As a result, in a semester class of fifteen weeks, the Gospel of John may be studied for thirteen or fourteen weeks, followed by a brief study of 1 John, and the letters of 2 John and 3 John get mentioned on the last day of class along with the last part of 1 John. In some commentaries, one introduction covers all of John's letters. In this series of Bible Study Guides, each of the three Johannine books that are included in the General Letters has its own introduction.

My first detailed exposure to 1 John came when I translated the book in first semester Greek. In that class, I not only learned Greek—I also learned much about the book of 1 John. But, as one would expect, the typical introductory questions were not covered in my Greek class.

Introductory Matters

One of the first questions to be answered in the study of 1 John is, "What kind of literature, or what genre, is the book?" In that it has no salutation, personal greetings, or closing greetings, the book of 1 John is not technically a letter, even though it is usually identified as such. The lack of personal names is highly unusual. Hebrews is another New Testament book that does not include the name of the author and does not identify the recipients.

The book of 1 John addresses a problem with false teachers. The false teachers are usually identified with Gnosticism because of the repeated affirmations in the book concerning Jesus having come in the flesh. Seen from another vantage point, the book focuses on the nature of Christian fellowship. It also reinforces the Christian's victory over sin through Jesus Christ and the need to keep God's commandments—especially the commandment to love one another. The conclusion of the book reminds that the Christian has assurance of salvation, power over and protection from sin, a genuine loving fellowship, and eternal life.

The book is theologically rich in its description of Jesus Christ, the assurance of salvation by faith, the demand for Christian obedience that delivers one from sin, and the necessity of brotherly love. John uses the word "know" twenty-seven times. The book is grammatically uncomplicated, yet it presents profound truths in simple language. The book contains much repetition and frequently uses contrasts. (See Stylistic Features below.)

The book is difficult to outline with its multiple recurring themes. One of the better ways to outline the book is to recognize that the main ideas are woven together in patterns that are somewhat repetitive. Many outlines of the book find it difficult to maintain the chapter division that was superimposed on the book centuries after it was written. (A suggested outline of the book appears later in this introduction.)

Author

Although there is no internal reference to the author, the tradition of the early church Fathers is unanimous that John the Apostle authored the book. That evidence includes allusions made by Clement of Rome (AD 90) and quotations from Polycarp (AD 110-140) and Justin Martyr (AD 150-160). The Muratorian fragment (AD 180) and Irenaeus (d. AD 202) attributed the book to John and Tertullian quoted the book.

Many contemporary scholars recognize similarities in the writings attributed to John including vocabulary and grammar. There is no reason to deny that John authored all five books traditionally attributed to him—the Gospel of John, 1 John, 2 John, 3 John, and Revelation.

Date

The date of the writing of the book depends on one's view of authorship. The traditional view places the book near the end of the first century and maintains that it was authored by John. That timeframe corresponds to the development of Gnostic thought and the doctrinal problems that are reflected in the book, especially the questions concerning the divine and human natures of Jesus Christ. Some would date the book a little earlier. There is little to be gained by the speculations that attempt to determine the order of the writing of John's books. The books of 1 John, 2 John, and 3 John are so named on the basis of their length.

Recipients

The absence of specific personal references may indicate that the book was intended for a number of churches, all of which were experiencing problems with the false teachings described in the book. The book is traditionally associated with the churches of Asia Minor, with Ephesus suggested as the place of composition. If John wrote 1 John and Revelation in the same approximate time period, it may be helpful to note that John was in exile on Patmos when he wrote Revelation.

Historical Setting

The book must be understood against the backdrop of its historical setting. The use of hypothetical statements likely reflects some of the misunderstandings and false teachings. "If we say..." (1:6-10) and "he who says...." (2:9; 4:20) are examples.

The content of the book gives hints about the false teachings that were threatening the church near the end of the first century. Some were denying the incarnation of Jesus; some were suggesting alternative methods of salvation, especially related to secret knowledge; some Christians were involved in inappropriate lifestyles, perhaps as a result of a dualism that separated body (flesh) and spirit. The instructions concerning brotherly love may reflect a tendency toward exclusivism—that those with knowledge looked down on and rejected others among the believers. The teachings of Gnosticism tended toward two conflicting polarities: asceticism or self-denial (whatever the body wants is evil and must be prohibited), and hedonism or self-gratification (the body is totally separate from the spirit, so whatever the body wants is acceptable).

That this book was written in the context of Gnosticism seems certain. Jesus is the Christ (2:22; 5:1); Jesus is the Son of

God. Jesus Christ came in the flesh (4:2); therefore Jesus was seen, heard, and made manifest.

Glossary

Docetism. From the Greek word, *dokeo* (to seem), this teaching said that Jesus only appeared to be human, that his body was not human, either because it was a phantasm or because its substance was not physical but heavenly. Therefore, he only seemed to suffer. This was a significant teaching among the Gnostics.

Gnosticism. From the Greek word, *gnosis* (knowledge), this teaching denied the identity of Jesus in his humanity with the divine Christ. Gnostics thought that they possessed special knowledge. They were dualistic in thought, separating the body (flesh) from the spirit. Because of this dualism, they taught that Jesus could not have a human nature and a divine nature simultaneously.

Stylistic Features

In most New Testament literature, it would be beyond the scope of a brief introduction to mention stylistic matters. However, in the case of 1 John, an awareness of these factors is important. One must recognize John's use of repetition, contrast, foreshadowing, formulas, and synonyms. John uses repetition antithetically, through both restatement and contrast. In some parts of the book, ideas or themes are introduced and then developed with repeated use of the same word. At times, John anticipates a new subject in the final clause of the previous paragraph, but the clause has no apparent connection with the paragraph it concludes (3:10, 3:24). John's frequent use of certain phrases (if we say, the one saying, I write, we know, hereby we know) is a type of repetition that provides emphasis but is not particularly helpful for outlining.

Purpose

As has been said, the book was written to combat a problem with false teaching. The specific doctrinal focus had to do with the belief that Jesus could not simultaneously have dual natures, being both divine and human. This teaching is often associated with Gnosticism. One result of the false teaching was that the relationship between the spiritual realm and the physical realm tended to be blurred. This tendency explains the focus of the book on the Christian's victory over sin: both through forgiveness by the propitiation of Jesus and through walking in the light and doing right as those born of God.

The book has several purpose clauses: "in order that...." These clauses suggest a practical purpose for the book: that the book would bring the recipients joy, encourage godly living, encourage them to love one another, and give assurance of eternal life.

Applications of the book today, those that focus on the message of the book, will challenge the contemporary church (1) to think carefully about how cultural thought patterns are easily integrated into the Christian faith, (2) to question any emphasis on correct teaching that excludes lifestyle and relational matters, and (3) to reject a merely intellectual Christianity.

Structure and Outline of the Book

Because of the stylistic characteristics mentioned above, the structure of the book is difficult to discern. The use of terms of address may be helpful in outlining, but in some passages a too frequent repetition presents difficulties (2:28; 3:2, 7, 13). The book is constructed by building idea upon idea with frequent repetition and intertwining. Rather than following an outline that meets the expectations of Western thought patterns, the book often seems to resemble a spiral, or perhaps a tower where upper pieces of the construction mirror lower pieces.

Phrases that are repeated in the book include the following: [#1] "This is the message" (1:5; 2:7; 3:11). The phrase does not continue in the second half of the book. The message is identified as "God is light," "the old command," and "love one another." [#2] "I write" (1:4; 2:1, 7-8, [12-14], 21, 26; 5:13). The absence of this phrase in Chapters 3-4 eliminates it as a helpful tool for paragraphing. [#3] "By this," or "this is how" (2:3, 5; 3:10, 16, 19, 24; 4:2, 6, 9, 13 ,17; 5:2). The uses of this phrase are often grouped together; the phrase does not seem to function as an organizational tool. [#4] Terms of address such as "children" (2:1, 18, 28; 3:7) and "beloved" (2:7; 3:2, 21; 4:1, 7, 11).

Because of the unique difficulties in outlining the book, a detailed outline is provided below. Paragraphs and subparagraphs are identified based on internal indicators, especially the use of terms of address. The same outline is provided in small segments at the beginning of the chapters, but seeing the outline in its entirety should be helpful. Many outlines of the book have been developed. The outline included here is one option among many.

There is general agreement about the individual paragraphs. What is less easily seen is how the paragraphs should be fitted together. In the outline provided below, larger sections of the book are identified and titled according to the general content of the sections.

The outline is helpful for identifying themes that are repeated throughout the book: false teaching and Jesus' identity, victory over sin, keeping God's commands, loving one another, practicing righteousness, and the relationship between the last two items. The book concludes with a summary conclusion.

Brief Outline

Here is a suggested shorter outline, followed by a more detailed outline.

1:1-4	Prologue
1:5 – 2:17	Fellowship with God through God's provision and commands
2:18-3:24	False teachers went out from us and rejected the truth
4:1 – 5:12	False teachers reject Jesus' nature and God's nature, despite sure testimony
5:13-21	Epilogue

Detailed Outline
PROLOGUE
1:1-4, prologue, introduction, correctly understanding Jesus as the Word of Life, purpose for writing

FELLOWSHIP WITH GOD; VICTORY OVER SIN
1:5-10, fellowship with God who is light, walking in light deals with the sin problem and gives victory over sin, continual forgiveness on the basis of Jesus' blood [combining deity and humanity]
>1:5-6, Fellowship with God implies continual cleansing of sin
>1:7-10, Sin is continually forgiven as one walks in the light

JESUS CHRIST BRINGS VICTORY OVER SIN; KNOWING GOD DEMANDS KEEPING HIS COMMANDS
2:1-6, Sin is forgiven by Christ who serves as Advocate and propitiation, knowing God demands keeping his commands
>2:1-2, The goal is not to sin, but when one sins victory is still possible because Jesus is sin sacrifice for all the world
>2:3-6, knowing God and keeping commands means walking as Jesus walked

KNOWING GOD AND KEEPING HIS COMMANDS (LOVE)
2:7-17, keeping his commands includes the command to love one another
>2:7-8, the command to love is both old and new
>2:9-11, love reveals whether one walks in light, walking in light demands brotherly love
>2:12-17, summary and application, restatement of purpose
>>2:12-14, assurance of fellowship is the power for overcoming evil
>>2:15-17, to know God and keep his commands, one must avoid the world (worldliness)

FALSE TEACHERS AND TRUTH
2:18-27, a correct understanding of Jesus
>2:18-21, the "last hour" false teachers (antichrists) have left the church, truth is confirmed through the anointing
>2:22-25, the false teaching denied Jesus in the flesh, denied fellowship with God, and denied the promise of eternal life
>2:26-27, the anointing confirms the truth and rejects false teaching

TRUE TEACHING: GOD'S CHILDREN ABIDE IN HIM AND PRACTICE RIGHTEOUSNESS (CONFIDENCE)

2:28-3:1, true teaching, children of God, abiding in him means doing right

    2:28-29, abiding in Christ gives confidence at his coming; being God's child implies doing right

    3:1, God's love makes us children, rejected by a world that does not know him

GOD'S CHILDREN DO NOT SIN

3:2-6, Because God's children will be like him, purity is required, abiding in him means no sin

    3:2-3, believers are children of God and are therefore like him

    3:4-6, abiding in him means one does not make a habit of sinning

TRUE TEACHING MAINTAINS THE COMMAND TO LOVE ONE ANOTHER

3:7-20, Practicing righteousness demands loving the brothers

    3:7-10, the one abiding in Christ and born of God does not practice sin

    3:11-20, abiding in him means that we should love one another

        3:11-12, the story of Cain and Abel speaks to the need for brother love

        3:13-15, lack of brother love is like hatred and denies one eternal life

        3:16-18, love is manifested through good deeds as one walks as Jesus walked

        3:19-20, brotherly love gives confidence before God

SUMMARY: RESULTS OF OBEYING THE TRUTH, FAITH AND LOVE (CONFIDENCE)

3:21-24, summary and application

    3:21-22, answered prayers

    3:23, believe in Jesus and love the brothers

    3:24, the result is fellowship with God, evidenced by the presence of the Holy Spirit

FALSE TEACHERS AND THE NATURE OF CHRIST
4:1-6, identifying the false teachers
> 4:1-3, false teachers are identified by whether they confess Jesus as Christ in the flesh
> 4:4-6, false teachers, spirit of truth and spirit of error, identified by relationship with the world

GOD'S NATURE IS THE BASIS FOR THE COMMAND TO LOVE
4:7-5:4, God's nature is love, and love identifies God's children
> 4:7-10, knowing God through love, born to be his children
> 4:11-14, brotherly love as a response to God's love brings fellowship with him
> 4:15-16, love is impossible without faith in Jesus
> 4:17-19, the heights of love, mature love casts out fear
> 4:20-5:4, God's command to love demands obedience which exhibits love for God

JESUS' NATURE MAKES POSSIBLE VICTORY OVER SIN AND OVER THE WORLD THROUGH FAITH
5:5-12, Faith is the victory over the world
> 5:5-6, Those believing in Jesus overcome the world
> 5:7-8, faith is established by reliable testimony
> 5:9-12, God's testimony is sure, those who accept his testimony have fellowship with Him

CONCLUSION
5:13-21, summary and application
> 5:13-17, assurance of the victory and ultimate salvation
> 5:18-20, confidence through faith; God protects; the Christian belongs to God; real fellowship brings eternal life
> 5:21, concluding verse, warning against sin

Resources

The Greek text used is the 27th edition of *Novum Testamentus Graece* which is identical with the 4th revised edition of *The Greek New Testament*. Other tools I find helpful include my Greek concordance (Moulton and Geden), Greek lexicons (Arndt and Gingrich, and some older lexicons), and Greek vocabulary studies (*Theological Dictionary of the New Testament*;

Dictionary of New Testament Theology, Colin Brown; and Moulton and Milligan).

Many English translations have been consulted. Those consulted most frequently include the English Standard Version (ESV), New English Translation (NET), and New International Version (NIV).

Various commentaries have been consulted. I always enjoy and find helpful the works of Stott. Roberts' commentary on the Letters of John has also been helpful. The on-line studies prepared by Utley reflect my own training about how to approach the biblical text.

1 John 1

[Note: it is suggested that the student review the introductory materials in this guide before beginning individual preparatory reading and analysis.]

CONTENT

The outline and paragraphing included in the Content section of each chapter are intended to serve only as suggestions or guides. The student is encouraged to read the text carefully and identify the paragraphs and subsections within each paragraph as part of his or her own study. The division of the biblical text into paragraphs is more difficult in 1 John than in many other books. The sections included in the outline below are identified in many studies and translations.

Outline of the Chapter
1:1-4   Introduction, the Word of Life
1:5-10 This is the message: fellowship, God is light, walking in light

Note: some would continue the paragraph through 2:2 based on similarity of theme, but the phrase "my little children" in 2:1 makes understanding the paragraph as 1:5-10 the preferable option.

Overview of the Chapter

The prologue in 1:1-4 is much like the prologue in John's Gospel (1:1-18). The prologue not only serves to introduce the book, it also presents theological truths related to the humanity of Jesus Christ. Verses 3 and 4 provide a purpose statement for the book.

The theme of the second part of Chapter 1 is victory over sin—made possible through fellowship with God who is light, through walking in the light, through the continual cleansing of Jesus' blood, and (anticipating the second chapter) because Jesus Christ serves as Advocate and as propitiation for the sins of the world.

Several verses in this chapter help one understand the false teaching John was combatting. Jesus had a physical presence and reality that was observed, seen, felt, and heard. The purpose of writing is fellowship between believers and with God. Fellowship with God, which includes forgiveness of sins, cannot be separated from lifestyle and one's commitment to live for God. Knowledge alone is not enough. To know God is to obey him.

STUDY HELPS

1:1-4. This section begins with one extended sentence in Greek, vv. 1-3a. The primary verb in the sentence is "proclaim" (*apaggello*, announce) in v. 3. The word is associated with the apostolic message (*kerygma*). The message of the apostles and the early church was that Jesus came to earth and took upon himself the nature of humanity (Phil 2:6-10). In the prologue of 1 John, four clauses describe the contents of the proclamation: "what was from the beginning," "what we have heard," "what we have seen with our eyes," "what we have looked at and touched with our hands." The message proclaimed clearly included the incarnation of the Christ (Christ is the Greek word, equivalent to the Hebrew word, Messiah). Verse 2 is inserted parenthetically. Verses 3 and 4 can be described as a purpose statement for the book.

The emphasis of the prologue is on the humanity of Christ. The descriptions affirm his human nature while affirming also his preexistence, "from the beginning." He is described as "Word of Life" and "his Son Jesus Christ." The prologue speaks about Jesus' preexistence, clearly paralleling the introductory verses in John's Gospel. Jesus was existent (imperfect tense, continuing past action) with the Father from the beginning. The phrase "from the beginning" can refer to the creation, but in the context of 1 John it is more likely a reference to the beginning of Jesus' life on earth. The other three clauses ("have heard," "have seen," "observed and touched") relate to Jesus' life on earth. John is asserting the humanity of Jesus, verifiable through the empirical senses. "Touch" (*pselaphao*) can mean "closely examined by feeling" (cf. Luke 24:39).

Here the pronoun "we" refers either to the Apostles or the early witnesses of Christ. The word is used over fifty times in the book. In some verses, it seems to refer to the shared experience of the author and the recipients. Context is always the determining factor for understanding what a word means and how it is used.

The description of Jesus as the "Word (*logos*) of Life" is important in the context of 1 John. The word *logos* was widely used in Greek philosophy. The presence of *logos* makes everything logical. *Logos* is the basic philosophical underpinning of logic. God sends both a written word and a living word. The *logos* of God gives true life (*zoe*). *Zoe* is usually spiritual life as opposed to biological life (*bios*). In John's writings, *zoe* consistently refers to spiritual life (cf. John 14:6).

1:2. Jesus, the Word of Life, was revealed (*phaneroo*, made manifest, brought to light). This phrase emphasizes Jesus' incarnation. The life that is revealed is described as eternal life. John has seen and thus testifies and announces (*apaggello*, proclaim) the eternal life that was with the Father and is now revealed. The verb is repeated (1:2, 3) and is the primary verb in the extended sentence. The eternal life that was with the Father refers to Jesus Christ, providing a clear statement of his preexistence.

1:3. "What we have seen and heard" repeats verbs from v. 1. The repetition connects v. 3 to v. 1 after the parenthesis of v. 2. Proclaim is the main verb of the sentence. The proclamation or announcement has the purpose of making possible fellowship with God's people and fellowship with God. This fellowship is with the Father and with his Son.

1:4. "These things" either refers back to what has been written in vv. 1-3 or looks forward to the entire book. "We write" may be an editorial "we;" the text provides no internal evidence concerning others who were with John when he wrote. The preferable reading for the textual variant is "our" joy instead of "your" joy. The reference is likely to both the author and the recipients. The purpose for writing is that joy may be made full. In 2:1, the purpose for writing is to avoid sin.

1:5-10. The message John is announcing, a message that has also been announced by others, is the message heard from "him." Jesus has been heard, the message has been heard. John heard the message from Jesus directly, and indirectly from the Father. The third person pronouns, "him," throughout the section are ambiguous, but no major biblical teaching is altered on the basis of reading God or Jesus. The use of the singular, "sin," communicates an abstract concept. The plural, "sins," is personal and specific.

The description of the message begins in this way: "God is light and in him (that is, in God) is no darkness." The "message" refers to the rest of the chapter which as a unit presents a complete thought. Because God is light, and his unchanging character is light (1 Tim. 6:16), the presence of darkness is impossible with God. In the context, light is a metaphor for purity, darkness for sin. The claim to have fellowship while walking in darkness and not according to truth is an impossibility. Fellowship is possible only by walking in light and in fellowship, with the result that Jesus' blood cleanses from all sin. Sin (darkness) is a constant reality that is defined by truth. The recognition and confession of sins (plural, personal) coupled with God's faithfulness and righteousness brings about the forgiveness of sins (personal) and cleansing from every form of unrighteousness. To deny that we sin makes him (God) a liar, therefore denying that God is pure light. Such denial fails to honor the truth of God's word.

1:6. "If we say…." The third class conditional statements that John uses to present his arguments seem to refer to the false teachings (1:8, 10; 2:4, 6, 9). An alternative view is that the statements describe misunderstandings of the recipients. John's use of the plural first person, "we," is interesting. Later in the book, the phrasing will more often be, 'if anyone says….." To claim fellowship with God, the One who is light, and at the same time walk in darkness is a falsehood and evidence of failure to practice truth. Fellowship is not based on knowledge and words; fellowship is based in actions—practicing the truth.

1:7. "If we walk in the light" is a first class conditional statement, considered to be true. A good translation for such statements is "when." "Walk" is a New Testament metaphor for "live." Walking in light as God is in the light means fellowship (*koinonia*, sharing, participation) with other Christians and cleansing from sin by the blood of Jesus. God is light; God is in the light. Fellowship with other believers is essential to walking in light. Failure to practice truth and lack of fellowship with others (Chapter 2, lack of love) makes fellowship with God impossible.

The basic problem is clear. How can sinful human beings have fellowship with a sinless God? It is possible because those walking in the light have their sins continuously cleansed by the blood of Jesus. Jesus' sacrificial death was atonement so that sins are forgiven. The blood of Jesus cleanses from all sin (singular, without the article, every kind of sin). The cleansing is continuous.

1:8-9. To deny sin (third class condition, indicating potential action) is self-deceiving and untruthful. Sin is a reality in the life of every human being, even those who are Christians. To confess sins (third class condition, potential action) results in forgiveness of sins and cleansing from unrighteousness. "Sins" is plural and specific. Each individual can be forgiven of the specific sins committed. The basis of forgiveness is not one's confession, but the faithfulness of God. Sin must be confessed (*homologeo*, to say the same thing). We must say the same thing about sin in our lives as God says. We must acknowledge sin. "He is faithful and righteous" refers to God the Father. God is introduced as righteous, in contrast to human unrighteousness. The theme of righteousness will be developed in Chapter 3.

1:10. If we say that we have not sinned, we make the faithful God a liar. Such is an inherent impossibility. "His word is not in us" parallels and is synonymous with v. 8, "the truth is not in us." In Chapter 1, the message, the word (*logos*), and the truth are used as synonyms.

1 John 2

[Note: it is suggested that the student review the introductory materials in this guide before beginning any individual preparatory reading and analysis of the text.]

CONTENT

The outline and paragraphing included in the Content section of each chapter are intended only as suggestions or guides. The student is encouraged to read the text carefully and identify the paragraphs and subsections within each paragraph as part of his or her own study. In the study of 1 John, the division of the biblical text into larger paragraphs or thought units is often difficult. The outline provided here reflects the basic building blocks of the biblical text but does not attempt to group the subsections and suggest larger paragraphs.

Outline of the Chapter

2:1-2	Christ our advocate and expiation to deal with sin
2:3-6	Knowing God and keeping his commands means walking as Jesus walked
2:7-8	A command that is both old and new
2:9-11	Love and walking in the light
2:12-14	Assurance of fellowship that overcomes evil
2:15-17	Avoid the world to know God and keep his commands
2:18-21	False teachers, truth confirmed through the anointing
2:22-25	False teaching: denying Jesus in the flesh, denying fellowship, denying eternal life
2:26-27	Anointing, truth, reject false teaching and abide in truth
2:28-3:1	True teaching, abiding in him means doing right

[Note: the last section is included in the Study Helps in Chapter 3.]

Overview of the Chapter

The recurring themes in 1 John make outlining difficult. Paragraphing may be choppy; longer paragraphs are hard to identify. Chapter 2 continues to explore and expand the themes of Chapter 1, at least through 2:17. Many commentators identify the beginning of a new major section in 2:18 with the focus on specific teachings being spread by the false teachers. I have indicated the possibility of a transition by using a double-space in the outline above.

Summarizing 1:5-2:17, whether one has fellowship with God and knows him can be evaluated: walking in light, truthfulness (word and deed), confession of sin, obedience, presence of love of God, in him, brotherly love, victory over evil, separation from the world.

The "if we say" of Chapter 1 becomes "the one saying" in Chapter 2.

"The last hour" uses wording specific to John and is not literal. "Hour" is used also in John's Gospel: my hour, a coming hour. The idea being communicated is that of completeness or fulfillment. This very specific meaning and use should not be confused with Paul's "last days" or "last times."

"Antichrist" is used only by John (1 John 2:18, 22; 4:3; 2 John 7). The characteristic of an antichrist is that he does not confess that Jesus has come in the flesh.

STUDY HELPS

2:1-2. The use of a term of address by the author, "my children" (*teknion*), may indicate the beginning of a new paragraph. An affectionate description may also be used as a way to connect with the readers personally, or the descriptions may reflect John's advanced age when he wrote. John uses two different words: *teknion* (2:1, 12, 28; 3:7, 18; 4:4; 5:21) and *paidion* (2:14, 18), both of which are translated "children."

The use of the aorist subjunctive (so you may not sin) likely refers to periodic sinful acts. The present tense often indicates continual sin. In 3:6 John writes that one who lives in Him does not practice sin (present tense), and that the one who makes a habit of sin "has not seen him or known him." The purpose of a Christian is to avoid sin as completely as possible, not to make a practice of sin. Nonetheless, Christians do sin (if anyone sins, third class condition communicates potential action). If someone sins, we have an advocate (*parakletos*). Here the Paraclete is not the Holy Spirit but Jesus Christ the righteous one. This verse is the only place in the New Testament where Jesus is described with this word. The word was used to describe a legal advocate or lawyer. Jesus Christ comes alongside us and serves as intercessor. The description of Jesus as "the righteous one" introduces a theme that will be reappear several times in the book. Righteousness and justice are translations of the same Greek word; the context helps make the choice of which English word to use.

2:2. Jesus is the atoning sacrifice (*hilasmos*, propitiation, expiation) for sin. The power of his sacrifice extends not only to Christians (our sins) but is sufficient for the sins of the world, meaning "all people." Here the word "world" refers to people, as in John 3:16.

2:3-6. "By this we know that we have known him, if we keep (*tereo*) his commands." Assurance is possible for the Christian. That we have known Jesus is something we can know assuredly, based on actions (2:3, 5; 3:24; 4:13; 5:2, 13). "To know" is not mere mental knowledge; it includes personal experience and relationship. Assurance is based on knowledge, with the assumption that knowledge leads to obedience (keep his commands). Keeping his commands is a choice—it is not automatic. "If we keep his commands" uses the conditional subjunctive.

2:4-5. To claim to know him without keeping his commands is an impossibility. Such a claim is a lie and evidence of the absence of truth (cf. 1:8-10). Perhaps some false teachers were asserting (perfect tense) that they had an advanced and complete knowledge of Jesus. Whether one knows Jesus or not depends on keeping his commands. Verses 4-5 make the same claim, in the negative of v. 4 and in the positive of v. 5.

For the one who keeps his word, the love of God has been perfected (*teleioo*, to make complete). "The love of God" can refer to God's love for us or our love for God. The former would mean that God's loving purpose is brought to completion in one who obeys; the latter would mean that one's love for God is demonstrated and completed in obedience.

2:5-6. By this we know (cf. 2:3) that we are in him: the one claiming to abide (*meno*) in him walks as he walked. "To walk" means "to live." "Abide" is used frequently by John (e.g. 2:10, 14, 17, 19, 24, 27; 3:6, 9, 14, 15, 17, 24; 4:12, 13, 15, 16). This section of text, considered as a unit, makes clear the necessity of obedience. One cannot disobey and reject the word, the commands, the truth, and at the same time affirm to know him and to be in him. The pronouns in this section of text are ambiguous, referring either to God the Father or to Christ the Son. The covenant that God extends without placing preconditions is conditioned on human acceptance, response, and obedience. Obedience is not the means of salvation but is the prerequisite. Obedience involves the way one lives, imitating Jesus, walking as he walked.

2:7-11. "Beloved" seems to mark a new paragraph or thought unit that contains two distinct subsections: vv. 7-8 and vv. 9-11.

2:7-8. John writes about a command that is both old and new. The use of contrast is common in John (see Introduction). Commands was plural in vv. 3-4, here it is singular. The command is not new; it is the command they had (imperfect, were having) from the beginning. The command was not new in terms of time or content. They had heard it before. The specific command John writes about is not specified in vv. 7-8. The context of vv. 9-11, connecting brotherly love with light and hatred with darkness suggests that the specific command concerns brotherly love. See also 3:11, 23; 4:7, 11, 21.

Perhaps the command was old because it was part of the Old Testament Law (Lev. 19:18), with "from the beginning" referring to Creation. The command also part of the teachings of Jesus (John 13:34), "from the beginning" referring to beginnings in Christianity. The second option is preferable, understanding that the imperfect past tense (you were having from the beginning) refers to the experience of the readers. For other uses of the phrase, "from the beginning," see 1:1; 2:24; 3:11.

The command is also new. The description of the command as new is usually understood in terms of quality or extent—to love as Jesus has loved us presents a new dimension (John 13:34; see also 1 John 3:16). "The command is true in him and in you." This sentence likely means that it is being lived out. The command was lived out by Jesus; it is being lived out by the readers. It is true because darkness is going away (*parago*, depart, leave) and the true light is shining, because of Jesus' coming. Darkness and light are themes carried forward and repeated from 1:5-7. Darkness is the absence of light. The presence of light dispels the darkness. In 1:6, darkness referred to sin. Sin is not passing away. A better understanding is that ignorance is passing away. God is light. Jesus is light (John 1:4, 5, 9; 8:12). Truth and knowledge have come.

2:9-11. These verses are grammatically simple. One who claims to be in the light while hating his brother is still in darkness (until now). Hatred belongs to the darkness. The present tense shows an ongoing attitude.

2:10. Brotherly love is connected with light. Brotherly love is not emotion; one who loves presents no cause of stumbling to a brother. The phrase could refer to the fact that one who loves does not stumble, but in the context, it seems better to understand that love presents no cause for stumbling.

2:11. One who hates his brother is in darkness and walks (lives) in darkness. Darkness makes sight impossible. In this verse, darkness has blinded the one who hates. Without sight and in blindness, such a one does not know or understand where his actions will eventually lead (where he is going). Notice the contrasts—light and darkness, love and hate do not coexist.

2:12-14. "Children" is from *teknion* (2:1). Why these verses are addressed to children, fathers, children (*paidion*), and young men (*neaniskos*), and what distinctions may be intended, are not clear. John is addressing believers. All of these verses can be applied to all Christians. Fellowship with and knowledge of the Father and of the Son brings forgiveness of sins, strength through the word, and victory over evil and the evil one.

Does John write "that" or does he write "because"? The six phrases may be purpose clauses, but I prefer to read them as statements of fact (following the NET). John writes certain truths to encourage his readers.

2:12. That, your sins have been forgiven because of his name.

2:13. That, you have known the one who has been from the beginning. This phrase must be understood as a parallel reference to 1:1, referring to Jesus (cf. 2:3). This phrase is repeated in v. 14.

That, you have overcome (*nikao*) the evil one. This phrase is repeated in v. 14.

2:14. That, you have known the Father.

That, you have known the one who has been from the beginning.

That, you are strong, the word of God abides in you, and you have overcome the evil one. In the context, the point is clear that strength depends on the word of God.

2:15-17. To know God and keep his commands, one must properly understand "the world." Here, "the world" does not refer to people but to the physical world and its values. The world to which John refers is passing away (*parago*, this verb is used in v. 8 with reference to darkness). That which remains (*meno*, exists, abides) forever is the one who does God's will.

Do not love the world. Do not love the things in the world. For one loving the world, the Father's love is not in him. Everything in the world—fleshly lust, the lustful look, and pride—is from (ablative of source, generated by) the world. Things in the world would include the material universe, possessions, passion and lust, power, prestige, and pride. Pride is related to arrogance (cf. Jas. 4:16). Such things do not come forth from the Father. The things of the world are going away. That which remains forever is God's will, and those who do his will.

2:18-21. "Children" is from *paidion*. Verse 18 marks an obvious paragraph break, beginning a new section. "Last hour" is uniquely Johannine. "Hour" is John's word for a certain season or proper time. The phrase here should not be confused with Paul's "last days" or "last times." To apply this phrase to Jesus' return goes beyond what the text says or demands. Here the reference is not future but present. The last hour has come; it is present.

John is the only New Testament writer who uses the word "antichrist" (1 John 2:18, 22; 4:3; 2 John 7). In 2:18, the word is anarthrous (without the article). To insert the idea of "antichrist" into texts where the word is not used is presumptuous. You heard (past tense) that antichrist is coming (the present is used to express the future); now what you heard predicted has come to pass and many antichrists have appeared. Fortunately, John does not leave us guessing about the identity of antichrist (4:2-3). Antichrist is characterized by the denial that Jesus came in the flesh and is from God. Antichrist is teaching against Christ as revealed by God. The false teachers that John is opposing are described as "antichrist" because of what they are teaching about Jesus, teaching that is contrary to the apostolic testimony. For John's readers, antichrists have already appeared. Based on the context, it seems the prediction of antichrist was associated with "last hour." Therefore, John writes that the appearance of antichrists indicates that the last hour was present for John's readers toward the end of the first century.

2:19. John further describes the antichrists. The antecedent of "they" in v. 19 is the antichrists in v. 18. The antichrists went out from the believers because they were not "of us." Fellowship is broken by false teaching. Those who bring false teaching are not "of us," and the church that firmly holds to the message of Jesus will find that such persons soon leave.

2:20-21. "You have an anointing from the Holy One." The second phrase is either "you know all things" or "you all know," depending on which textual variant is read. Both readings are powerful opposition to Gnosticism. Knowledge is available to every Christian; all things can be known so there is no body of "reserved knowledge" limited to the elite. For more on "the anointing," see comments below on v. 27.

John's readers know the truth and can readily discern the truthfulness or falsity of the false teachers. All that is necessary is to compare a particular teaching to the truth since no lie (falsehood) is of the truth.

2:22-25. These verses clearly refer back to v. 18 and antichrist, the denial that Jesus is the Christ. The larger paragraph is in vv. 18-27, with "children" introducing a new section in v. 28.

The false teachers are not truthful in their denial of Jesus as the Christ. The antichrist denies both the Father and the Son. To deny the Son is to deny the Father (not have the Father). To confess the Son is to have the Father. Denial and confession illustrate John's use of contrasts. Fellowship with the Father depends on fellowship with the Son, and vice versa.

2:24-25. What John's readers had heard from the beginning must abide in them. Accepting the teaching they heard from the beginning means that they abide in the Son and in the Father. Eternal life is the promised result of abiding (5:13).

2:26-27. John is writing about the deceivers, the false teachers, those who bring a false message concerning Jesus' identity, "the antichrist." The "anointing" from the Holy One (2:20) refers to the Holy Spirit. The focus is not on the means (Holy Spirit) but on the result (knowledge). The result of the anointing is knowledge of the truth about Jesus. When the anointing they have received remains in them, they do not need teaching (no need for the false teachers). The anointing teaches or communicates truth. Since "anointing" is not John's common way of referring to the Holy Spirit, these verses may reflect the teaching of the Gnostics that valued higher knowledge. The work of the Holy Spirit through the apostles and through Scripture brings adequate and reliable truth. Since the anointing teaches, the only other option for understanding the anointing seems to be the word of God, and referring to the Bible as the "anointing" is even less likely than a reference to the Holy Spirit.

The anointing teaches about all things, the anointing is true and is not a lie. Spiritual truth comes from God. Follow the teachings received through the anointing—abide in him.

2:28-3:1. See the Study Helps in Chapter 3.

1 John 3

[Note: it is suggested that the student review the introductory study guidelines and materials in this Bible Study Guide before beginning any individual preparatory reading and analysis.]

CONTENT
The outline and paragraphing included in the Content section of each chapter are intended to serve only as suggestions or guides. The student is encouraged to read the text carefully and identify the paragraphs and subsections within each paragraph as part of his or her own study. The outline provided here sets forth the individual thought units but does not attempt to group the subsections into larger paragraphs.

Outline of the Chapter
2:28-3:1	True teaching, children of God, abiding in him means doing right
3:2-6	God's children will be like him; therefore, purity is essential, abiding in him means no sin
3:7-10	The one abiding in Christ and born of God does not practice sin
3:11-20	Abiding in him and doing right means loving one another
3:21-24	Answered prayers, believe in Jesus, love the brothers [fellowship in the Holy Spirit]
3:24-4:6	Spirit of truth and spirit of error

Overview of the Chapter
      This chapter suggests that one result of the false teaching was the tendency to separate salvation from lifestyle. Abiding in him means doing right, seeking purity, not practicing sin, and loving one another.
      The teachings in 3:2-10 have been a source of much misunderstanding because of the strict standard set forth. Christians sin (1:7-10) but Christians do not make a practice of sinning. The use of the present tense in 3:2-10 holds the key: Christians

are not in the habit of sinning. This chapter, as all of Scripture, must be read in context. The goal is that we not sin (2:1-2). In Romans 6-7, Christians are delivered from sin so that sin no longer has power. In Galatians 5, walking in the Spirit avoids works of the flesh. In 1 John, Christians sin but their lives are not characterized by constant sin. Because of the continual cleansing made possible by Jesus' blood, assurance of salvation is possible. Assurance is not based on sinlessness.

The rest of the chapter (3:11-20) deals with the relationship between abiding in him, righteousness, and brotherly love.

In this study, 3:21-24 is understood as a separate thought unit on the basis of the term of address in 3:21, "beloved."

STUDY HELPS

2:28-3:1. Various commentaries begin the new paragraph in 2:28, 2:29, or 3:1. Based on the term of address, "children," and the repetition between v. 27 and v. 28, the outline presented here seems preferable. These three verses are a distinct unit, but they function as introduction to teachings in 3:2-10. Christians must "abide" in him. Christianity is both a response and an effort.

As has been the case throughout the book, the antecedents and specific references to the third person pronouns are often difficult to identify. The context helps determine the best option. When Jesus appears, we can be confident without shame. Confidence (*parrhesia,* boldness) is based on knowing God, Jesus, and the message. The appearing is not in question, only the timing of his appearing. The coming (*parousia*) refers to Jesus' return.

2:29. He (Jesus) is righteous (cf. 2:1, 28; 3:7). Based on that truth, everyone who practices righteousness is born of him (God). A reference to God the Father seems the best option for the second pronoun (3:9; 4:7; 5:1, 4).

3:1. John transitions from the idea of being born of God to being children of God. That we can be called children of God is evidence of the Father's great love. Our status as children is not theoretical, it is real. "Such we are." This phrase is not in some later manuscripts and is not in the KJV, but it is well-attested and rated "certain" by UBS[4]. "World" is used in the same way as in 2:15-17. There is a great disconnect between the world and God's children, just as the world rejected Jesus (John 1:11).

The world rejects Christians as it rejected Christ, for lack of knowledge.

In 1 John, the word for love is always agape (verb, *agapao*). However, in the Gospel the two words (verb, *agapao/phileo;* noun, *agape/philia*) are used synonymously (cf. John 5:20; 11:3, 36; 12:25; 15:19; 16:27; 20:2; 21:15-17). God has given us his great love, calling us his children. This description is given by God himself. The idea of being God's children is essential to the context of 2:28-3:10.

3:2-10. The frequent use of vocatives, "Beloved," results in short, choppy grammatical units. The first section (3:2-6) is controlled by the "Beloved" in v. 2. The second (3:7-10) is introduced by the use of "children" in v. 7.

3:2-3. Even though we are children of God, the ultimate result of "what we will be," is not yet apparent. "When he appears" is parallel to 2:28. When Jesus appears, we will be like him. What John means when he affirms that "we will be like him" must be determined by the context. A primary application has to do with our practice of righteousness and purity. We will be in his likeness, image restored, and we will recognize this truth because we will see him as he is. This hope causes the Christian to seek purity (to purify himself) because he (Jesus) is pure.

3:4-6. These verses point to one truth: in him there is no sin. Abiding in him has implications for purity. The three verses sequence the argument. (1) One who practices sin practices lawlessness, v. 4. (2) Jesus appeared to take away sin, in him there is no sin, v. 5. (3) No one who abides in him sins; no who sins has seen him or known him.

The present tense in v. 4 must be noted. The subject is the practice or habit of sin, referring to one's lifestyle. Lawlessness refers to one's attitude toward law more than one isolated transgression. One transgression is sin, but John's point is broader. Sin is an attitude that does not care about God's commands (2:3).

Jesus appeared to take away sins, referring to his Incarnation. His sacrificial atonement (2:2) made possible "no sin" (2:1). Jesus came to take away sins (v. 5) and to destroy the devil's works (v. 8). "In him there is no sin." In him there was no sin, his sinlessness made possible his perfect sacrifice. In his presence, sin cannot exist.

No one who abides in him sins (present tense, continuous action). One must read this verse in the context of 1 John. Seeing him and knowing him are antidotes to sin.

3:7-10. The one abiding in Christ and born of God does not practice sin. To deny sin is self-deception (1:9-10). To practice sin while claiming to abide in Christ is also deceptive. The antidote to deception is truth. "One who practices righteousness is righteous, just as he is righteous." Christians have a declared vicarious righteousness based on Christ's righteousness applied in our lives. We are declared righteous (justified) through the faith of Christ (cf. Rom. 3:21-26). Our justification does not finalize faith but is rather the beginning of faith. Christ's vicarious death does not negate the necessity of our faithfulness. Faith responds. Righteousness is not the means because it is not meritorious, but it certainly is a measure. "The one who practices righteousness is righteous."

Verse 8 is set in contrast to v. 7. One practicing sin (contrasted with righteousness) is of the devil. Sin is consistent with the devil's nature, he has sinned from the beginning. Jesus appeared, the Son of God appeared, to destroy the works of the devil. Jesus did that with his sacrificial atonement and the shedding of his blood for our cleansing.

One born of God does not practice sin. This combines the two thoughts presented thus far: we are children of God, we seek purity as we abide in him and do right. What is the seed that abides in one born of God? Suggestions include God's Word (Luke 8:11), the Holy Spirit, the divine nature (2 Pet. 1:4), and Christ as the seed (Gal. 3:16). The last makes good sense in the context—he abides in us, although the third option also has much to commend it. The result is that one born of God cannot sin (practice sin continually), either because of Christ's presence in him or because of his changed nature.

3:10. This verse summarizes the section. Those who are children of God are easily distinguished from those who are children of the devil on the basis of their practice (righteousness vs. sin). The last phrase in v. 10 is an example of John's method of anticipating a new subject in the final clause of a paragraph, when the clause has no apparent connection with what has gone before (see also 3:24). Children of God will also be distinguished by brotherly love.

3:11-20. Abiding in him and doing right means loving one another. Several themes are repeated in v. 11. "The message" occurs only in 1:5 and 3:11. What follows is a part of the message which the readers had heard from the beginning (cf. 1:1; 2:7, 24). That message was primarily about Jesus and his identity. The message included instructions for how to live, specifically for escaping darkness and living in light (cf. 2:9-11 and 3:14). Here John says that the message is "that we should love one another." One of the interesting challenges in reading 1 John is to try to understand how and why John balances or contrasts the doctrinal message and the ethical implications of the message. Loving one's brother is connected with righteous living (3:10, 14). This theme will continue through Chapter 4, with a parenthetical interruption in 4:1-6.

3:12. Cain is given as an example of one who did not exhibit brotherly love. The reasons given are that he was of the evil one, because Cain's deeds were evil, and because Abel's deeds were righteous. This description echoes themes and concepts John has previously used in the book.

3:13-15. Not only does the world (2:15-17; 3:1) not know us; the world hates us. The reaction of the world is not a cause of surprise. The value systems that guide the Christian are distinct from the value systems of the world. Brotherly love is an evidence of having passed (*metabaino*, to change location, to depart or leave) from death into life. Lack of brotherly love signifies that one remains (*meno*, abides) in death. John uses corresponding contrasts—darkness and light, love and hate; death and life. The death and life John is referring to are spiritual or eternal. One who hates his brother is a murderer (like Cain), and eternal life does not abide in any murderer.

3:16. Many know John 3:16. Would that we would also learn 1 John 3:16! "By this we know" is a favorite formula of John. How can one know and understand love? Love is ultimately understood in the fact that Jesus laid down his life for us, and that we should follow his example (2:6), that we should lay down our lives for the brothers. In the midst of John's teachings about love (2:9-11; 3:10-24), it is important to note that John is not writing about love generically. He is writing about a very specific love—brotherly love, love for the brothers. There is nothing in these verses that speaks to the relationship of a Christian to unbelievers, unless it is to note that we are not to love the world and the values reflected by unbelievers in the world, that unbelievers in the world do not know us because they do not know God, and that in fact the world often hates Christians. Understanding "the world" through personification, it may be that the world in some way hates Christians, but equally valid is the understanding that "the world" refers to unbelievers.

3:17-19. Laying down one's life as Jesus did may or may not require dying. It certainly requires sacrifice, otherwise nothing is laid down. Love is not measured by what I give, but by what is left over. Love is not measured by what I give to other Christians, but by how much I spend on myself. John presents a practical application. One who has physical possessions and goods, sees a needy brother, and closes his heart, cannot affirm that God's love abides in him. With such lack of love for fellow believers, one cannot claim to imitate God's love for us, and one cannot accurately claim to love God.

3:18. Love is not only expressed verbally; love results in actions. One who reads the text carefully is likely surprised by the mention of "truth." John is using synonyms: word and tongue, deed and truth. We seldom consider truth in this way, as synonymous with deeds. What one considers true is reflected by what one says and also by what one does.

3:19-20. These two verses present a number of translation and interpretation problems. "By this we will know that we are of the truth...." Some interpreters apply the phrase "by this" only to the verb "we will know;" others apply it to both verbs, "we will know and we will assure (*peitho*) our hearts." Some think the phrase, "by this," most naturally looks backward, but the grammatical construction seems to point forward. Truth is repeated from v. 18. It is true that brotherly love gives confidence before God, but is that what these verses are saying?

Peitho (active voice) means to convince, to appeal or persuade, to please or win over, and to pacify or smooth. Translators are divided about the exact meaning in this text. The object of the verb is "our heart." Does "heart" refer to conscience, thinking, or will? Based on the context, heart likely refers to the conscience, since our consciences condemn us (v. 20). Our consciences are convinced, reassured or set at rest.

What sets our consciences at rest? The conviction or assurance that when our consciences condemn us, God is greater than our conscience and knows everything. Thus, the meaning is something like this: "This is how we know that we practice truth and find reassurance and rest for our consciences when our consciences condemn us: God is greater than our conscience and knows everything." The focus is on God's understanding and not on God's judgment. The instructions of vv. 16-18 are difficult to follow. Who is ready to give up life and sustenance for other Christians? Who has complete compassion for other Christians? We often feel that we could have or should have done more. God knows our motives, our intentions, and our abilities (Heb. 4:12-13). This truth is a cause for hope and not a cause for dismay. We know truth and assure our consciences not because of what we do, but because of who God is.

3:21-24. In this Study Guide, a new grammatical section is begun on the basis of "beloved." Is the thought continued or repeated? Do we have another example of John's tendency to insert an anticipatory and unrelated clause at the end of a section (3:10 anticipating 3:11-20; 3:19-20 anticipating 3:21; 3:24 anticipating 4:1-6)? This section (3:21-24) is best understood as the conclusion of the larger section (2:18-3:24) dealing with the false teachers. A new section dealing with the false teachers will begin in 4:1 (4:1-5:12).

3:21-22. If our conscience does not condemn us, we have confidence with God. The "if" clauses in v. 20 and v. 21 are third-class conditions, possibility that is not always present. Only sometimes are our consciences satisfied so that we approach God confidently to receive what we ask. Such confidence is based on keeping his commands and doing the things that please him. Believers receive what they ask because their hearts are in tune with what pleases God. The frequently heard idea that God promises believers unlimited answers to their prayers fails to address the primary condition—that our requests are consistent with God's eternal plan and purpose.

3:23-24. His command (cf. 1:5 and 3:11) is to believe in Jesus and love one another. One command (singular) encompasses two parts. God has commanded two things which are merged into one command. God commands belief and brotherly love. The referent for "he" is God based on the phrase "his son Jesus Christ" in v. 23. The one who keeps these commands abides in God and God in him. Abiding requires obeying—believing and loving.

3:24. The chapter concludes with the inclusion of a phrase that has no apparent connection with what has gone before, but clearly introduces the next section of text. (See Introduction, Stylistic Features.) We abide because of obedient faith and brotherly love. We also know we abide by the Spirit whom he has given us. The mention of the Spirit should remind the reader of the "anointing" in 2:20, 27.

1 John 4

[Note: it is suggested that tin he student review the introductory materials this guide before beginning individual preparatory reading and analysis.]

CONTENT

The outline and paragraphing included in the Content section of each chapter are intended to serve only as suggestions or guides. As always, the student is encouraged to read the text carefully and identify the paragraphs and subsections within each paragraph as part of his or her own study.

<u>Outline of the Chapter</u>

3:24-4:6	Spirit of truth and spirit of error determined by teachings about Jesus' nature
4:1-6	How to identify false teachers
4:7-5:4	God's nature is love and love identifies God's children
4:7-10	Knowing God through love, born to be his children
4:11-14	Brotherly love as a response to God's love brings fellowship with him
4:15-16	Seeing God through love, love is impossible without faith in Jesus
4:17-19	The heights of love, mature love casts out fear
4:20-5:4	God's command to love completed by obedience, exhibiting love for God
[**5:5-12**	Belief in Jesus gives victory over the world, the testimony is sure]

<u>Overview of the Chapter</u>

    Much of this chapter returns to themes that were presented previously in the book. Who is in fellowship with God? Who shares in the fellowship of believers? How does one ascertain truth? Who speaks for God authentically? Such questions relate to walking in light, obeying God's commands, separating oneself from the world, faith in Jesus, recognizing the human and divine nature of Jesus Christ, rejecting false teachers, understanding truth, practicing righteousness, and loving God's children. This list includes things that must be believed and things that must be practiced.

The first section (4:1-6) relates to Jesus' nature as one having come in the flesh. What one teaches about Jesus is the test to distinguish false teachers and false teaching. This teaching relates also to truth and error.

The rest of the chapter (4:7-19) focuses on God's nature: God is love. The command for brotherly love is based on God's nature, and that fact that God's children become participants and share in the nature of the Father.

The connection between 4:20-21 and 5:1-4 is strong. For this reason, these verses are treated as a separate paragraph, and the Study Helps on 4:20-21 will be included in the Study Helps for Chapter 5.

STUDY HELPS

4:1-6. Despite the mention of the Spirit, clearly referring to the Holy Spirit, in 3:24, in this section "spirit" is used in the sense of a human being. In v. 6, the contrast between the "spirit of truth" and the "spirit of error" likely refers to individual persons (cf. "of the truth," 3:18) although some interpreters make the phrases references to the Holy Spirit and Satan. The point is that one can examine prophets (teachers) to determine who are the false prophets. Prophet is used in the generic sense of teacher without reference to predictions.

4:1-3. Christians often follow personalities, seek spectacular displays, and desire popularity. Some teachers were claiming to have a message from God. All teachings should be tested (*dokimazo*, examine) before accepting them (1 Thess. 5:20-21). Not every teacher should be believed. It seems that those who had left were still claiming to speak for God, despite their denial of Christ's humanity. The spirits (their messages) can be tested and discerned. The spirit that is from God (spirit of God, likely not a reference to the Holy Spirit in this context) confesses Jesus as having come in the flesh. The spirit that does not confess Jesus is not from God, but is the spirit of the antichrist. This statement repeats and clarifies 2:18-23. The question of Jesus' nature was an important deviation in the teaching of the false teachers, identifying them with the Gnostics of John's time. That Jesus is both divine and human is a major theological truth that is essential to the gospel. Antichrist denies Christ. The readers had heard that antichrist was coming and was already in the world (2:18-19). Antichrist is identified by the teaching about Jesus that is contrary to apostolic testimony and Bible teaching. Nothing more is said or can be said biblically, although detailed complex theories have been developed by inserting antichrist into texts where the Bible says nothing about antichrist.

4:4-5. "Children" suggests a new grammatical unit. The last phrase of v. 3, "already in the world," seems to remind John of the subject of vv. 4-6. "World" in 4:3 refers to the present physical realm. What is the relationship of a Christian to the world? Those who are from God overcome them (referring either to those in the world, or more probably to the false teachers), because "greater is he who is in you than he who is in the world." In 3:24, John affirmed that God abides in the believer. "He who is in you" refers to God. "He who is in the world" likely refers to Satan. "They are from the world" refers to the false teachers. They share the viewpoint of the world, their thoughts and teachings are generated in the world, they are participants in the world with its lusts and arrogance. "The world hears them" either personifies the world or refers to those in the world. One way to identify false teachers is to evaluate who listens to them.

4:6. One who knows God listens to those who are from God, those who are not from God do not listen to those who are from God. By observing and evaluating who listens to which teachers, one can know the spirit of truth and the spirit of error. Believers recognize true teachers by the contents of the message—faith in Jesus and brotherly love.

4:7-19. "Beloved" marks a new section. The command (3:23) included faith in Jesus and brotherly love. The nature of Christ can be used to distinguish the false teachers (4:1-6). The nature of God can be used to distinguish false teachers (4:7-19). False teachers deny the Son and thus deny the Father (2:22-23).

(Formatting note: Because of the length of this section, the subparagraphs are separated and begin without indention.)

4:7-10. Those who are God's children know God and are characterized by love. While the text speaks of love generally, the context of 1 John suggests that the topic continues to be brotherly love, "let us love one another." The source of love is God, "love is from God." The absence of love indicates that one does not know God, the one who is by his very nature love, "God is love." John uses the word *agape* for love. *Agape* love is not compassion or emotion. *Agape* love is measured by intentional actions (3:16-18).

4:9-10. God showed his love for us by sending his Son into the world so we might live through him. A comment is necessary concerning the translation of the Greek word, *monogenes*, sometimes translated as "only begotten." *Monogenes* means one of a kind or unique. The translation "only begotten" may imply a time of beginning. Contemporary translations more frequently use the translation, "one and only" (cf. John 1:14, 18; 3:16, 18). The word is used in the book of Hebrews of Isaac, meaning unique son of promise, although Isaac was not the only son Abraham begot (Heb. 12:17).

Because God's action so clearly demonstrated the nature of love, and that he by nature is love, love is not defined by how we love God. The essence of love is not our love for God, but his love for us, sending his Son to be the atoning sacrifice (2:2) for our sins.

4:11-14. "Beloved" may mark the beginning of a new unit, but the topic clearly continues without interruption. Because of God's love for us, we should love one another (3:16). God's love for us cannot be doubted. Brotherly love as a response to God's love brings us into fellowship with him so that we abide in Him and He in us. Reading between the lines, we should understand that the actions and attitudes of the false teachers were unloving.

4:12. God who is unseen can be loved with *agape* love (cf. John 1:18). *Agape* does not depend on visible presence. When we love one another, God abides in us and his love is perfected (*teleioo*, to bring to completion) in us (2:5; 4:17).

4:13-14. The mutual abiding relationship can be known because he has given us his Spirit (3:24). Verse 14 summarizes vv. 7-14, suggesting that the two units identified in the outline should be understood as one, despite the insertion of "Beloved" in v. 11. John is writing and testifying about what he has seen (1:1-3). God sent Jesus as Savior of the world (2:1-2). God sent Jesus to redeem the world, referring to people in the world.

4:15-16. Although the Study Helps are being presented in smaller subunits or subparagraphs, the themes that are repeated in vv. 7-19 suggest a single larger section. John has just affirmed the mutual abiding relationship based on love (v. 12) and the presence of God's Spirit (v. 13). Now he says that the mutual abiding relationship is based on faith in and confession of Jesus as the Son of God. These three statements are not "multiple choice." The correct answer is "all of the above." All of these descriptions are essential to the mutual relationship and indwelling. When one sees God as he is, with an understanding consistent with God's nature, one also understands that love is impossible without faith in Jesus and God's presence with us. Believing and acting upon the truth concerning the person and work of Jesus is an essential part of love.

4:16. On the basis of what has been said, now we know and believe God's love for us, demonstrated in sending Jesus and giving us the Holy Spirit. Literally, the text says "we have known" and "we have believed." God has acted purely out of love, having no other option because that is what he is by nature. "God is love." One who is a child of God and has the nature of God will also be characterized by love, "abiding in love." Such a one abides in God and God in him.

4:17-19. "By this" refers to at least vv. 15-16, and more probably to the entirety of the section beginning in 4:7. The phrase is used frequently in this section (4:2, 6, 9, 13, 17). On the basis of what has been said, love is brought to completion (4:12). The completion of God's love in us gives confidence (*parrhesia*, boldness, 2:28; 3:21; 5:14). in the day of judgment. As He is, so we are in this world. Because God is love, our lives are characterized by the same nature.

4:18-19. Building on the idea of confidence in v. 17, John observes that love does not produce fear (*phobos*). In this context the word should be understood to mean terror, not reverence. In fact, there is no terror in love, perfect love (the love of God perfected, 2:5; 4:12, 17) casts out such fear. Fear anticipates punishment. One who is fearful has not experienced the love of God brought to completion in his life. Such a one is not perfected (brought to maturity) in love. "We love because he first loved us." The verb, "we love," should not have a direct object according to the manuscript evidence. We love, we are able to know love, because of God's love for us.

4:20-21. For the Study Helps on these verses, see 5:1-4.

1 John 5

[Note: it is suggested that the student review the introductory materials in this guide before beginning individual preparatory reading and analysis.]

CONTENT
The outline and paragraphing included in the Content section of each chapter are intended to serve only as suggestions or guides. The student is encouraged to read the text carefully and identify the paragraphs and subsections within each paragraph as part of his or her own study.

Outline of the Chapter
4:7-5:4   God's nature is love, and love identifies God's children
- **4:7-11**   Knowing God through love
- **4:12-16**   Seeing God through love
- **4:17-19**   The heights of love
- **4:20-5:4**   God's command to love is applied through obedience

5:5-12   Belief in Jesus gives victory over the world, made certain by testimonies
5:13-17   Assurance of the victory and ultimate salvation
5:18-20   Confidence through faith
- God protects
- The Christian belongs to God
- Real fellowship brings eternal life

5:21   Conclusion, warning against idolatry

Overview of the Chapter
   As explained in the overview of Chapter 4, the section in 4:20-5:4 is being treated as a paragraph. The comments on 4:20-21 are included below.
   In modern translations, there is general agreement about the division of this chapter into grammatical units. The conclusion of the book begins in 5:13 with a passage that is well known:

"I have written these things that you might know you have eternal life."

The question of the "sin unto death" and the "sin not unto death" in 5:16-17 has presented difficulties to some students. The context is the key to understanding this text.

STUDY HELPS

4:20-5:4. John once again cites a potential situation (1:6, 8, 10; 2:4, 6). The third class condition indicates a possibility: Someone may claim to love God while hating his brother. Such a one is a liar. The section in 4:20-21 reflects 2:9-11 and 3:14-15. One who does not love a brother whom he has seen cannot love God whom he has not seen (4:12). The command (3:23) says that one who loves God should also love his brother. We understand that the command says more than that, but John is addressing the conflicting claim that would separate love for God from love for the brothers. John consistently uses "brother" as a reference to other believers.

5:1-4. John presents certain situations to illustrate his teachings (2:29; 3:3, 4, 6, 9, 19; 4:7; 5:1). The example John gives in 5:1 is a real situation. John uses the singular (whoever) but the principle applies to all believers. Those who believe that Jesus is the Christ are God's children (born of God). Those who love the Father automatically love the children of the Father. The fact that Jesus is the Christ is the core of the gospel and is the principal objection to the teaching of the false teachers. That Jesus is the Christ is also shown to be central to receiving the Spirit and understanding brotherly love.

5:2-4. These verses repeat a major theme of 1 John. We are to love God's children; Christians are to love one another. How does one measure that dynamic? How do we know that we are doing that? The first time John mentions love, it is to say that love is expressed by obedience to God (2:3-6). Love for God's children is evident and made sure when we love God and keep his commands. Love for God's children is expressed by loving God and obeying his commands. The true believer loves God and therefore obeys the commands. Loving God and obeying the commands is evidence of love for God's children. By loving God and obeying God's commands, the true believer loves God's children.

The essence of loving God is to keep his commands, and those commands are not weights (*barus*, a burden). Everyone born of God overcomes (*nikao*, 2:14) the world. "World" refers to the system that opposes the Christian system of belief and values. What is the victory that overcomes the world? Is it love? Is it the Spirit? No, it is our faith! Why? Because faith in Jesus is the foundation that makes possible the abiding presence of God through his Spirit and the practice of the faith of Jesus.

5:5-12. The one who overcomes the world is the one believing that Jesus is the Son of God. The content of our faith and the basis of our practice is Jesus as the Son of God. Victory is made possible by the certainty of the testimony. Jesus came by water and blood – not by water only but by the water and the blood. Many interpretations have been given of the significance of water and blood: (1) the water and blood which flowed from his side at his crucifixion, (2) references to baptism and the Lord's Supper, (3) purification and redemption, related to #2 but using different descriptions, (4) his birth and his death, and (5) his baptism and his crucifixion. Without extensive explanations of why the first four are inadequate, my preference is for the last. At his baptism Jesus was commissioned for his ministry, and at his death he fulfilled that commission. Jesus was shown to be both divine and human on these two occasions

5:6-8. A number of textual problems exist in vv. 6-8 regarding the readings of the manuscripts. A full treatment of these questions is beyond the scope of this Bible Study Series. The reader with a great interest in the question will readily find help in other resources.

"The Spirit is the witness because the Spirit is the truth." The Spirit was present at Jesus' baptism and throughout his ministry. Jesus promised to send the Spirit after his departure (John 14-16). in John 20, Jesus gave the Spirit after his resurrection. These three are witnesses: the Spirit and the water and the blood, and they agree. Three witnesses were sufficient to establish truth.

5:9-12. The testimony of God is greater than the testimony of men. These verses are reminiscent of John 5:36-39. The testimony of God, his testimony about his Son, refers to vv. 5-8, and perhaps more broadly to the testimony John is providing as an eyewitness (1:1-3). God also gave testimony about his Son at his baptism and at the transfiguration: "this is my beloved Son." The one who believes in Jesus as the Son of God has this testimony, such a one is "of the truth." The one who does not believe makes God a liar because he does not believe the testimony that God himself gave about his Son. The testimony continues: God has given us eternal life in his Son, and this life is possible only through the Son of God. No other option exists: Jesus was both divine and human. The one who does not accept that truth concerning the Son of God does not have eternal life.

5:13-17. This passage marks the beginning of the conclusion or epilogue. The overall theme is assurance of victory and eternal salvation. John has written to believers to assure them about eternal life (cf. 5:11-12): "that you may know that you have eternal life." This verse has parallels in John 20:31, and in the conclusion of the Gospel of John.

The repetition of the verb (*oida*, perfect tense of "to see," translated "to know") in 5:13-20 provides an interesting list of things believers can know: (1) they have eternal life, v. 13, (2) God answers prayers, v. 14, (3) God hears prayers, v. 15, (4) Christians are born of God and do not make a practice of sin, v. 18, (5) believers belong to God (are "of God"), v. 19, (6) the Messiah has come, v. 20, and (7) the things that are necessary to know the one who is true, v. 20.

5:14-15. Believers have confidence (*parrhesia*) concerning prayer. God hears and answers. Of course, prayer is also linked to God's will. We should pray one for another. This conclusion leads to vv. 15-16.

5:15-16. These two verses have been the basis of endless speculation. The basic question is this, "What is a sin 'not to death?'" Let me answer as briefly as possible. All sin results in separation from God, that is, all unforgiven sin is "unto death." All sin is serious. God is able to forgive, so any problem regarding forgiveness or lack of forgiveness must be based in human beings. God forgives sin when the sinner repents. God cannot and will not forgive sin when the sinner is unrepentant, not because of God's lack of power but because of God's nature. In the context, it seems that a sin "not unto death" is a sin about which the sinner is penitent and praying. Believers are encouraged to join their brother in prayer. A sin "unto death" is a sin for which the sinner is not penitent. Believers are not to make request for this. The context is prayer (vv. 14-15). Some prayers are inappropriate.

In the context, it seems that those who are committing the sin "unto death" are the false teachers who continually reject God's blessings and forgiveness that come only through Jesus Christ his Son. To reject God forever always results in spiritual death.

To summarize. When one sees his brother committing a sin "not unto death," a sin about which the brother is repenting, correcting, and praying, one should join his brother in asking for restored spiritual life. On the other hand, regarding the sin "unto death," one should not pray. The condition of the sinner in this case forbids such a prayer request. Could one pray for a changed heart? I would say yes, but a request for forgiveness and restored spiritual life is out of order. All unrighteousness is sin, but when a brother sins and confidently seeks God's forgiveness, requesting restored life, God hears and the sin is "not to death."

Some have attempted to connect these verses to the "unpardonable sin" about which Jesus taught (Mark 3:22-30 and parallels). No sin is unpardonable from God's perspective, as long as the sinner meets the conditions for forgiveness. Thus, the unpardonable sin is that sin for which the sinner will not repent and make restitution. That which makes a sin unpardonable is on man's part, not on God's part. With this understanding and definition, the sin "unto death" of 5:16-17 is unpardonable as long as the brother is unrepentant. I hesitate to connect the two contexts. Jesus was referring to a unique situation that faced the Jews he was addressing. Context is always the first key to understanding a passage.

5:18-20. Verse 18 has an incredibly difficult interpretation problem because of variant readings in the original text. A comparison of contemporary translations will show the difficulty. While the logical reference to "the one born of God" is to the Christian, in the second part of the verse the text appears to say that "the one born of God" keeps or protects the Christian so that the devil cannot touch him. The most likely reading is this: "We know that the one born of God does not sin, but the one born of God, he (God) keeps him and the evil one does not touch him" (NET). I believe the phrase, the "one born of God," refers exclusively to the Christian in this verse.

We know that one who is born of God does not practice sin (present tense, continuous action, cf. 3:4-10). Christians try to avoid sin (2:1-2). We also know "that we are of God" while the whole world is situated in the evil one, Satan.

5:20. "We know that the Son of God has come." This statement is an affirmation of the reality of the Incarnation. Jesus came so we could understand and know him who is true (God the Father). In the phrase "we are in the true one, in his Son Jesus Christ," the true one can refer either to God the Father or to Jesus. Both readings are possible grammatically and theologically. The former is more contextually valid, based on the continued affirmation that we abide in the Father. "This one is the true God and eternal life." We know that we have eternal life, because of who God is and what he has done in sending his Son Jesus Christ, the greatest evidence of his loving nature.

5:21. The book concludes abruptly. As such, the book hardly has the characteristics that would justify calling it a letter. The term of address, "Children," is repeated. The literal reading is easy enough: "guard yourselves from idols." "Idols" is used only twice by John (here and in Rev. 9:20). What kind of idolatry is John warning against?

Perhaps the best interpretation is to note that the Dead Sea Scrolls use the concepts of "idolatry" and "idol" to refer to "sin" generally. Perhaps the same synonymous usage occurs here, so that the admonition is to guard yourselves from sin.

Introduction to Second John

The letters of John, especially 2 John and 3 John, are often ignored in Bible study. In collegiate Bible classes, the letters of John are often included in a study of the Johannine corpus—a term that refers to all of the writings of John. As a result, in a semester class of fifteen weeks, the Gospel of John is often studied for thirteen or fourteen weeks, followed by a study of 1 John, and the letters of 2 John and 3 John get mentioned on the last day of class along with the ending of 1 John. In many commentaries, one introduction is provided to cover all of John's letters. In this series of Bible Study Guides, each of the Johannine writings included in the General Letters has its own introduction.

Author and Recipients

The author of the book refers to himself as "the elder" and addresses the book to an "elect lady" and her children. Stylistic features of the book, described in the Introduction to 1 John, argue that the author of 1 John is also the author of 2 John. The designation, "the elder," may refer to the fact that John served as a presbyter or overseer in a local church, although no other biblical references help to make that case. It is more likely that the word "elder" is used to describe one who is older and more experienced.

Regarding the "elect lady," either of the two words could be a proper name accompanied by a modifier, the Lady Eclecta or the Elect Cyria. That these are proper names is made less likely by the wording in v. 13: "your elect sister." The more likely option is that these words are descriptive, either of a specific person or in reference to a local church. The latter option is supported by the use of plural pronouns in vv. 10 and 12, and by the plural verb forms in vv. 6 and 8. However, the argument is not conclusive since John could be including the children with the elect lady. If "elect lady" is understood as referring to a local Christian church, the children would be members of that church. The "elect sister" would be another local church. (See 1 Pet. 5:13

for a possible parallel text where a local church is referred to with the feminine pronoun, "she.")

Characteristics and Theme of the Letter

No internal evidence is available to help identify the date and place the letter was written. The historical context is sketchy. The letter deals with hospitality to missionaries. The book shares this focus with 3 John. The focus of 2 John is on the problem of traveling preachers who did not understand Scripture and brought heresy. The focus in 3 John is on the need to help traveling missionaries who help advance the gospel.

The focus on the truth can hardly be missed. The importance of continuing the truth is coupled with the importance of following the truth. Love must be "according to truth." John's focus on truth is also seen in warnings against the false teaching of the traveling missionaries. The purpose of the book should be related to the themes the author treats.

Hundreds of one-page letters (one sheet of papyrus) have been found, three of which are included in the General Letters (2 John, 3 John, Jude). Since this book has only one chapter, the outline of the book is included immediately before the Study Helps below.

Resources

See Introduction to 1 John.

2 John

[Note: it is suggested that the student review the introductory materials in this study guide before beginning any individual preparatory reading and analysis.]

CONTENT

The outline and paragraphing included in the Content section of each chapter are intended to serve only as suggestions or guides. The student is encouraged to read the text carefully and identify the paragraphs and subsections within each paragraph as part of his or her own study. Use your own Bible for this reading. The division of the biblical text into paragraphs is fairly standard in modern translations.

Outline of the Book
1-3		Salutation and greetings
4-11		Truth and love
	4-6	Christ's commandments
	7-11	Deceivers
12-13		Closing greeting

Overview of the Book

Much of what should be said about a book that has only one chapter of thirteen verses has already been covered in the introduction to the letter. The primary focus of the book centers on false teaching that was being spread by traveling preachers.

STUDY HELPS

1-3. The description of the author as "the elder" *(presbuteros)*, both here and in 3 John, means either that John was a church leader in a local church (elder, overseer, and pastor all referred to the same group of church leaders), or that he was an older person when he wrote the book. The various options concerning how the description of the recipient should be understood are explained in the Introduction. The letter is addressed to the "chosen lady" and her children.

In the Gospel of John and the book of Revelation, John clearly uses *phileo* (to love, to like, to be friends) and *agapao* (to love) as synonyms so that little if any distinction can be made. In 1 John, 2 John, and 3 John, he uses *agapao* exclusively. No easy explanation exists. Perhaps the church had come to understand that Christian fellowship depended on extending honor, dignity and worth to all, and that Christian fellowship was not dependent on mere friendships. A clear understanding of what it really means to "love" others would be equally helpful in the contemporary church where "love" often depends on emotion, warm feelings, or friendships.

Truth shows up frequently in 2 John, both in the specific use of the word and in references to the teachings. Truth is set in contrast to the false teachings. "To love in truth" can mean "to love genuinely," but with the multiplied references to truth in the book, the reading "to love in truth" is preferable as a translation, making clear the connection between love and truth (see vv. 4-6). John's love for the recipients is shared by all who know the truth.

Truth abides in Christians and will continue to be present forever. "Abide" is a favorite word for John (41 times in the Gospel, 24 times in the shorter books, 1 time in Revelation). The greeting is typical of the Greek letter form. The inclusion of "mercy" is noteworthy, appearing also in the greeting in the letter of Jude.

4-11. This section sets forth the relationship between truth and love and has two major parts.

4-6. John was glad to hear that some of the church members were continuing in the truth, according to the commandment received from the Father. The word "some" does not appear in the original text, but the genitive case construction is partitive: literally, "I rejoice that I found 'of your children' walking in truth." The implication is that some had strayed, perhaps because of false teachings. How John had heard this news is not clear. The most probable options are that he had received a letter or that he had received the news from traveling Christians. The "commandment received from the Father" perhaps refers to the commandment to love, the context relates the command to "walking in truth."

Verse 5. The description of the command as the one "we have had from the beginning" relates it to the command to love one another. In v. 7 the command relates to "Jesus Christ as coming in the flesh." This dual description of the command is parallel to 1 John.

Verse 6. Having requested that Christians love one another, John describes the love he refers to. What is love? Love is walking according to his commandments. Love is the "sign" of all true believers (John 15:33-35; 1 Cor. 13; Gal. 5:22; 1 John 4:7-21). This love is always *agape*, it is measured by obedience, lifestyle, and teachings. In the absence of the doctrines and commands which God gives, obedience, and consistent Christian living, love does not exist. In our day when false doctrines are often spread in the name of love, the connection John makes between love and truth is essential to the contemporary church. Love requires that we walk according to his commandments. The command is that you walk in "it." The reference is ambiguous. Grammatically, "it" can refer to truth, the command, or love. My preferred reading is "walk in truth" (see v. 4). The two occurrences of the phrase "walk in truth" enclose vv. 4-6. This construction is consistent with the focus of the letter on false teachings, and explains the transition to v. 7.

7-11. The reason it is important to "walk in truth" is because of the presence of many deceivers (*planos*, the verb means to wander, as in our word planet) in the world. "Deceiver" refers to those who wander from the truth. The specific kind of false teaching mentioned is that they do not acknowledge Jesus Christ as coming in the flesh.

A doctrinal problem in the early church related to how one should understand the nature of Jesus Christ, as both divine and human. Some denied the full humanity of Jesus. The dualism of Gnosticism separated spirit (God) and matter (flesh), arriving at the conclusion that Jesus could not be fully God and fully human. A group known as the Docetists said Jesus only seemed or appeared to be human, but that he was in fact spirit. Others said that the "spirit" came on Jesus at his baptism but departed before his death on the cross. The one who questioned Jesus' nature and his human existence is identified as deceiver and antichrist (literally, against Christ). Complex theories about the existence of one known as "The Antichrist" have been constructed on the basis of a few biblical verses that do not mention "Antichrist." In John's writings (see 1 John 2:18, 22; 4:3; 2 John 7), antichrists are those who deny Jesus' existence as human. Many people are surprised to learn that these are the only verses in the New Testament that describe antichrists, that the word is not used in 2 Thess. 2 with reference to the man of lawlessness, and that the word never appears in the book of Revelation.

Verse 8. "Watch yourselves" (*blepo*) means that Christians are responsible for being alert and watching out for error. It is possible to lose what has been gained. It is possible to forfeit the reward.

Verse 9. "Everyone who goes on ahead and does not abide in the teaching of Christ does not have God." Goes on ahead (*prosago*) suggests going beyond a limit. What the verb means in this context is clearly stated—it is the description of one who does not stay with the teaching of Christ. The phrase "teaching of Christ" has been much discussed. The phrase can mean the teaching Christ gave (subjective genitive), the teaching about Christ (objective genitive), or it can have an element of both (plenary genitive). The context must determine the meaning. In 2 John, the "truth" and the "teaching" are parallel concepts. False teachers do not teach truth. The deceivers with whom John is specifically concerned in 2 John are those who deny a specific truth about Jesus—that Jesus has come in the flesh. However, the principle set forth in the verse can be applied to any kind of false teaching, because truth demands that one walk in the commandments. The practical application is the same. False teaching means one does not have God, true teaching means one has both the Father and the Son (see 1 John 2:23).

10-11. When (first class condition) someone comes and does not bring this teaching (v. 9), do not receive him into the house. "The house" likely refers to a house church, although the reference could be to Christian hospitality and refer to the particular houses of Christians. Receiving a false teacher is prohibited; so is giving a greeting. Unlike the casual greetings of today, the first-century greeting usually implied acceptance and approval. Do not give any appearance of fellowship with such a person, lest you share (*koinoneo*) in the evil deeds. These verses are difficult to apply. What teaching must be brought? What details must be in place? What room exists for disagreements about peripheral matters? When should greetings be withheld? Everyone wants to be cordial and open to conversations and study. At the same time, Christian leaders must be cautious about being identified with heresy.

12-13. These verses are much like 3 John 13-14. "Paper and ink" is not literal, but refers to writing on papyri. John hopes to visit the church soon to speak personally. The greeting of v. 13 is likely from members of a sister church.

Introduction to Third John

Allow me to restate briefly the case for including a separate introduction to the letter known as 3 John. The letters of John, especially 2 John and 3 John, are often ignored in Bible study. In collegiate Bible classes, the letters of 2 John and 3 John get mentioned on the last day of class along with the last chapter or the last verses of 1 John. In many commentaries, one introduction is sufficient to cover all of John's letters. In this series of Bible Study Guides, each of the Johannine books that are included in the General Letters has its own introduction.

Author, Canonicity and Recipient

This letter is known as 3 John only because it is slightly shorter than 2 John. As in the second letter, the author of the book refers himself as "the elder." The letter has traditionally been attributed to John with few opposing voices.

Eusebius (4th century AD) classified writings as accepted, disputed, and spurious. He accepted 1 Peter and put Hebrews, James, 2 Peter, 2 John, and 3 John in the disputed category. The letter of 3 John was not as readily accepted into the canon as was 2 John.

The letter is written to Gaius, an individual who is otherwise unknown in Scripture, although three other persons in the New Testament are named Gaius.

Theme and Outline of the Book

The book shares with 2 John a focus on extending hospitality to missionaries. The focus of 2 John is on the problem of traveling preachers who brought heresy. The focus in 3 John is on the need to help the traveling missionaries who advance the gospel. The early church struggled with questions related to receiving and supporting traveling evangelists.

Three men are specifically named in 3 John. Gaius is commended for his hospitality and Diotrephes is condemned for his refusal to receive traveling preachers. The book is carried by Demetrius who also receives a commendation. References to these three men make up the bulk of this little book. The Gaius mentioned here is likely not one of the other three men who had the same name (Gaius of Macedonia, Acts 19:29; Gaius of Derbe, Acts 20:4; and Gaius of Corinth, Rom. 16:23; 1 Cor. 1:14). In 3 John is the only mention in the Bible of Diotrephes. John and Gaius may have shared a fairly close relationship, based on v. 4 which implies that Gaius was a convert of John, and on John's anticipation of seeing Gaius soon.

Since 3 John another of the one-chapter books of the New Testament, the outline of the book is included immediately above the Study Helps.

Resources
See Introduction to 1 John.

3 John

[Note: it is suggested that the student review the introductory materials in this study guide before beginning any individual preparatory reading and analysis.]

CONTENT
The outline and paragraphing included in the Content section of each chapter are intended to serve only as suggestions or guides. The student is encouraged to read the text carefully and identify the paragraphs and subsections within each paragraph as part of his or her own study. The division of the biblical text into paragraphs is fairly standard in modern translations.

Outline of the Book
1-4	Greeting
5-8	Commendation to Gaius
9-10	The bad example of Diotrephes
11-12	Demetrius is praised
13-15	Final greetings

Overview of the Book
    Much of what should be said about a book that has only one chapter of fifteen verses has already been covered in the introduction to the letter. The primary focus of the book has to do with how the church should evaluate and receive traveling preachers or missionaries. Thematically, the book is much like 2 John, only that in 2 John the concern is with false teaching, and here the problem is with the need to help faithful teachers.

STUDY HELPS
1-4. For comments on the identification of the author as "the elder," see 2 John 1-3. The letter is written to Gaius who is identified as "the beloved." This description is not uncommon in the plural, but is not often applied to individual believers in the New Testament. The description is used frequently in John's writings

(1 John 2:7; 3:2, 21; 4:1, 7, 11; 3 John 2, 5, 11). The beloved Gaius is loved "in truth." This letter continues the conjunction of love and truth that is seen in 2 John.

2-4. "Beloved" is singular in vv. 2, 5, 11. The greeting of a letter written in the Greek letter form often includes or is followed by a brief prayer or wish. The desire here is for physical prosperity and health consistent with Gaius's spiritual prosperity. Apparently, John has received information from traveling brothers who have testified to Gaius's faithfulness to the truth (literally, "to your truth"). This news gladdened John. Gaius was walking in truth, that is, according to the truth.

John frequently uses the phrase "my children" or "little children." In 3 John, this may suggest that Gaius was a convert of John, or at least that he had been instructed by John. The term reflects an affectionate relationship. John's joy was that his children walk in truth, even as Gaius was (v. 3).

5-8. John commends Gaius for the help he has provided for traveling brothers. John assures him that he is acting faithfully in whatever he does on their behalf, especially because they are strangers. The brothers whom Gaius had helped had testified about Gaius's love when they gave reports to the church. The phrase, "you will do well" (*kalos poieseis*) is literally translated in most versions, but was a Greek idiom that meant "please, kindly, or be so kind as to" and frequently preceded a request (*Moulton and Milligan*, 1972 reprint, p. 522). "Be so kind as to send them on their way in a way that is worthy of God." "To send them on their way" implies assisting them with their needs.

The reason for helping them is that they went out on behalf of "the Name" and do not accept anything from the unbelievers (Gentiles, pagans). The "Name" stands for the work of the gospel in the name of Jesus Christ. Many traveling evangelists depended on their hearers for support. Paul took pride in being able to preach without receiving help from his hearers. The traveling evangelists to whom John refers were worthy of support by Christians because they were not preaching for money. Often the only support they needed was hospitality. The traveling teachers were sacrificially involved in God's mission, and those who helped them would be working together with them and with the truth.

9-10. After commending Gaius, John has words of condemnation for a certain Diotrephes. John had previously written about this to the church—apparently the church where Gaius attended. This writing may refer to 2 John. If it does not, the letter mentioned here is lost. Diotrephes is described as one who "loves to be first among them" and one who does not accept John's words. "To be first" means to have authority or rank above others. Here is an example of a church leader who wanted to lead by being a "power broker" or "gatekeeper." Diotrephes did not acknowledge John's teachings or authority as an apostle.

Therefore, John, if he is able to come (third class condition suggests uncertainty), will call attention to what Diotrephes is doing—bringing unjustified accusations against John and those with him. Diotrephes is not satisfied with speaking against John. He also refuses to receive the traveling brothers, and he forbids everyone else to do so. If any brothers challenge him, he puts them (not the traveling brothers, but those who would receive them) out of the church. He will accept no competition—he throws out all who disagree with him. The reader can probably think of multiple applications of these verses in the contemporary church that more often functions as a hierarchical institution than as a hospitable fellowship and family.

11-12. The third person mentioned in the book, Demetrius, is likely the one who carried the letter from John to Gaius. Some would include v. 11 with the paragraph in 9-10, seeing it as the logical culmination of the condemnation of Diotrephes. Others would include v. 11 with v. 12, maintaining that the praise for Demetrius begins in v. 11. Both options have merits. Clearly the verse serves as a bridge from the bad example of Diotrephes to the good example of Demetrius.

The principle is this: Do not imitate what is bad, rather imitate what is good. The one who does good is of God, the one who does what is bad has not seen God. One who has not seen God certainly does not know God. Christians must be able to discern good and bad, and they must choose their role models carefully.

Demetrius is testified to by all. It was customary for first century authors to call attention to the dependability of their carriers. However, the testimony supporting Demetrius came not only from Christians, but from the truth. This apparently means that Demetrius walked in truth, and if truth were to be called as a witness, the testimony would reflect Demetrius's commitment to truth. John adds his own testimony, speaking in the plural to represent those with him. The final comment is that Gaius knows the truthfulness of John's testimony.

13-14. These verses are much like 2 John 12. "Peace" reminds of the Hebrew *shalom*. It serves as a blessing. Sharing greetings was common in the closing part of a letter. Here the greetings are abbreviated and impersonal. "The friends here greet you. Greet the friends there by name." The words "here" and "there" are added for clarity in many translations but do not exist in the original text.

Introduction to Jude

My first detailed study of Jude was part of the same university Bible experience described in the introduction to the Letters of Peter. That in-depth introduction to the book of Jude came when I was an undergraduate student at Oklahoma Christian College in 1969. During the summer trimester, I enrolled in Dr. Raymond Kelcy's class on the General Letters. He was at the same time beginning work on a commentary over the Letters of Peter and Jude, a commentary that was to be part of the series published by the R. B. Sweet Company. When the commentary was published in 1972, I remember thinking that the notes I had taken in class were very much parallel to the contents of the commentary.

Even today, when I pull Kelcy's commentary off the shelf to check some aspect of the text, I fondly remember a summer spent in an intense study of the General Letters, and especially the studies in 1 Peter, 2 Peter, and Jude. My notes from that class have long ago been lost, but I still hear echoes of my beloved professor when I consult his commentary.

Introduction
The book of Jude addresses some of the dangers that confronted the church in the last half of the first century. Just as the book served as a warning to first century readers, so still today it reminds Christians of the continued danger of false teaching, rebellion, and ungodliness, and the certainty of future judgment. Christians must be always on guard to contend for the faith. The Christian's ability to combat the problems that confront Christianity depends on knowledge of the Bible, godly living, perseverance, and love.

Relationship to the Letter of 2 Peter
One of the more perplexing questions in the study of the letters of Peter and Jude is the relationship between 2 Peter and Jude. The two books treat the same themes, contains warnings that are essentially the same, and sometimes use the same or very

similar words and phrases. Numerous questions remain unresolved: which one was written first, why they have so many similarities, the possible existence of another document available in the early church from which both authors borrowed, whether the rebellious ones were Christians, and what it means that the heresy was future in 2 Peter and current in Jude.

Authorship

The author of Jude refers to himself as "a slave of Jesus Christ" and "a brother of James." Since the reference to James does not include any other descriptions, it is generally assumed that this James was well-known in the early church. The most likely option is James, the half-brother of Jesus, who was a leader in the early church and the author of the book that bears his name. If Jude is referring to James the half-brother of the Lord as his physical brother, then Jude was also a half-brother of Jesus. In this case, neither of Jesus' half-brothers chose to seek authority for their writings by citing their familial relationship to Jesus, perhaps out of humility. This factor is often cited as evidence against the possibility of pseudepigraphy, the practice of an author attributing his own work to a famous person of the past. Since Jude is relatively unknown in Scripture, Jude is not among the best options to be considered by a later writer wanting to give instant credibility to his work.

Date and Place of Writing

The date of the book cannot be determined based on internal evidence. To accept Jude's authorship places the book within Jude's lifetime, most likely in the latter half of the first century. How one answers the question about the date of Jude's writing also depends on how one understands the relationship of the book to 2 Peter. The book of Jude has only twenty-five verses, and almost two-thirds of those (16 of the 25 verses) have some similarity to verses in 2 Peter. The most likely options are that Jude cites 2 Peter or that both are citing a common source or sources. If Jude is quoting 2 Peter, the date of 2 Peter will help establish parameters for the date of Jude. Dating 2 Peter in the mid-60s requires that Jude be dated somewhat later, although conservative scholars usually date the two letters in the same general timeframe.

The contents of the book suggest a mid-first century date, perhaps not far removed from the dates of Paul's writings to Timothy, letters which also address problems with false teachers. The problems Jude addresses are more questions of morality than of specific doctrinal error. The book of Jude has a definite Old Testament flavor. A date in the mid- to late-60s presents a reasonable option, although the window of possibility includes the 60s, 70s, and 80s.

Acceptance into the New Testament Canon

A major problem for the acceptance of Jude into the canon was his use of non-canonical books such as *1 Enoch* and the *Assumption of Moses*. These books were known among the believers of the first century, but were not accepted as authoritative. What does it mean when an author uses a non-authoritative source to write an authoritative or canonical work? Is that possible? Does it imply that the books cited are authoritative, or even canonical? These were the questions the early church had to address. In parallel, one can note that the Old Testament cites uninspired sources and that Paul cited Greek writers.

The book of Jude was accepted early (Clement of Rome, about AD 94) and later disputed. It was listed among the disputed books by Eusebius, but was accepted in the church councils at Nicaea in AD 325 and at Carthage in AD 397. It was included in the Muratorian fragment in the late second century.

Recipients and Historical Context

The book of Jude, as other New Testament letters, is occasional literature, meaning that it was written for a specific audience in a specific situation. Who were the recipients, and what was their historical situation? One of the values of the book of Jude is that it helps the reader today to understand better the kind of problems that the early church faced. The situation Jude addresses was apparently characterized by lack of clarity with regard to authority in the church. Various problems had arisen with regard to the teachings of the church; Jude specifically mentions problems that had to do with increasing immorality and worldliness in the church. Doctrinal questions existed, the church was not effectively excluding false ideas and false teachers, and immorality was becoming more widespread. The resulting division was troubling the church. Some of the problems addressed may be associated with an incipient version of Gnosticism.

Purpose of the Book

The purpose of the book is related to the historical context. The author describes his desire to write about the common salvation (v. 3). Some have seen in this comment that he completely changed his mind and wrote about other problems when he became aware of the challenges facing the readers. However, it is also possible to see that his original intent was only focused more specifically by the news he received. (See comments on v. 3.) A quick overview of the book suggests that the author wrote to encourage believers, to help the readers contend for the faith (3, 20), to combat false teachers (18-19), to build up the recipients in the faith (20), to encourage prayer (20), love (21), and mercy (22-23), to motivate them toward expectant living and eternal life (21), to teach concerning those who have wandered and those who have doubted (22-23), and to reinforce assurance of salvation (24-25).

Resources

The Greek text used is the 27th edition of *Novum Testamentus Graece* which is identical with the 4th revised edition of *The Greek New Testament*. Other tools I find helpful include my Greek concordance (Moulton and Geden), Greek lexicons (Arndt and Gingrich, and some older lexicons), and Greek vocabulary studies (*Theological Dictionary of the New Testament*; *Dictionary of New Testament Theology*, Colin Brown; and Moulton and Milligan).

Many English translations have been consulted. Those consulted most frequently include the English Standard Version (ESV), New English Translation (NET), and New International Version (NIV).

Various commentaries have been consulted. The work by Kelcy has been helpful. I appreciate the studies prepared by

Utley because they reflect my own training about how to approach the biblical text.

Jude

[Note: it is suggested that the student review the introductory materials in this study guide before beginning any individual preparatory reading and analysis.]

CONTENT
The outline and paragraphing included in the Content section of each chapter are intended only as suggestions or guides. The student is always encouraged to read the text carefully and identify the paragraphs (and subsections within each paragraph) as an initial part of his or her own study. Use your own Bible for this reading; the division of the biblical text into paragraphs is fairly standard in modern translations.

Outline of the Book
1-2	Salutation and greetings
3-4	Reason for the letter
5-16	Judgment on false teachers
17-23	Warnings and exhortations
24-25	Doxology

Overview of the Book
     Much of what should be said about a book that has only one chapter of twenty-five verses has already been covered in the introduction to the letter. The primary focus of the book is to warn against false teachers. Those warnings are followed by some personal warnings and instructions before the concluding doxology. The author addresses the recipients as "beloved," but that may be a literary style more than an indication of a personal relationship between the author and his readers.

STUDY HELPS
1-2. That Jude, the half-brother of Jesus, is likely the author of the letter was explained in the introduction (see Matt. 13:55 and

Mark 6:3 where he is mentioned by name). The physical brothers (half-brothers) of Jesus were not believers until after Jesus' resurrection (John 7:5; Acts 1:14; 1 Cor. 9:5). Jude describes himself only as a slave of Jesus Christ and a brother of James. This James was a leader in the early church (Acts 15) and the author of the book of James, not to be confused with James the apostle, brother of John, of whose death we read in Acts 12.

The recipients are described as "loved, kept, and called." (The KJV has "sanctified" due to a textual variant in the Greek manuscripts.) "Kept" can be translated as guarded or protected. The three adjectives were well-known descriptions of God's servants, especially in Old Testament literature (see, for example, the Servant Songs of Isaiah, chap. 41-49). References to God the Father and Jesus Christ were common in the greetings of letters. To make the omission of a reference to the Holy Spirit in the greeting a matter of significance would be to overstate the case. The blessing of mercy, peace and love is unusual; the more normal expectation is grace, as in many of Paul's letters. The optative verb form, "may [they] be multiplied," is rare, although it appears also in 1 Pet. 1:2 and 2 Pet. 1:2.

These verses provide a typical greeting for a letter, but the content of the book is often characterized more as a sermon than as a letter. This suggestion is due, in part, to the absence of the characteristic closing greeting at the end of the book. Hundreds of one-page letters (one sheet of papyrus) have been found. Three are part of the General Letters (2 John, 3 John, Jude).

3-4. For comments on "beloved," see "Overview of the Book" above. A more literal reading of this section of text may be helpful: "While being quite diligent (*spoude*, eager, zealous) to write to you about our common salvation, I had a necessity to write to you exhorting to contend earnestly...." Diligence is also mentioned in 2 Pet. 1:5 where the same word is used, and the verb form is used in 2 Pet. 1:10, 15. "Contend earnestly" is an intensified form of a verb that was often used to describe athletic contests. In the context it appears that the need to contend arose from the presence of false teachers. The historical context can be described like this: when Jude learned about the presence of false teachers, he felt the need to write to encourage his readers to oppose the false teachers strongly. Obviously, false teachers teach error, but based on the contents of the letter, it appears that the greatest danger of the false teachers had to do with their ungodliness, influence, and bad example. In the New Testament, "the faith" usually refers to the body of Christian teaching (e.g. Acts 6:7; 13:8; Gal. 1:23; 3:23; Phil. 1:27; 1 Tim. 4:6). In the context of Jude, "the faith" was not only something to be articulated, it was something to be practiced.

Jude was planning, or perhaps had already begun, to write concerning the common salvation. In the midst of this process, for some unexplained reason, he felt the need to exhort his readers to contend for the faith. Whether this represents a change of subject or an expansion and more specific focusing of his original purpose is not clear. What did the phrase, "common salvation," mean to Jude's readers? What made the salvation common? Was it the exclusiveness of Christ, the gospel about Christ (2 John 7-10), the apostolic teachings or kerygma, the lifestyle of followers? How does "the faith once and for all given to the saints" relate to "the common salvation"? Is faith the basis and salvation the application? Is there a sequence, so that Jude felt the need to go back to the foundations of faith before continuing with the implications of salvation? While we confidently affirm that we have all the information we need, "the faith once and for all given," that does not mean that every question has been answered. Interesting questions remain that could perhaps help us better understand the intent of the author.

"The faith" has been given to the saints in a once-for-all action that is not to be repeated. The same concept is used to describe Christ's death (Heb. 9:26-28). The teachings were given by God and then were passed down (entrusted) from generation to generation. "Saints" is a typical way of referring to Christians.

In v. 4, Jude describes in more detail why he needed to write concerning "the faith." The need arose because of some who had slipped in (*pareisduo*), somehow secretly coming among the believers (cf. 1 John 2:18-19 for a parallel idea). What 2 Pet. 2:1 speaks of as future has now occurred. These had perhaps come from among the believers, or perhaps they had been accepted into the church while secretly holding false teachings or participating secretly in ungodly activities.

Regardless of their method of entry, they were deceitful (vv. 8, 10, 11-12, 16, 18-19). That they were marked (literally, written about) for condemnation may refer to false teachers generally. Such persons had already been condemned by Scripture. "Long ago" can be translated as "already" (see Mark 15:44). It is possible that Jude was referring to 2 Peter. The condemnation mentioned ("this condemnation") seems to refer to what follows.

The main problem Jude mentions with regard to the false teachers is that they are ungodly persons, turning (*metatithemi*, to exchange, to substitute, but in this context, to pervert or to distort) grace into immorality and denying Jesus Christ. "Ungodly" is a frequently used word in this book (v. 15). That grace can be used to give license is not a new problem (2 Pet. 2:19). This passage may refer to some type of sexual exploitation. Regardless, the false teachers were focused on themselves. They deny "Jesus Christ, our only Master and Lord" (cf. 2 Pet. 2:1). "Deny" can mean "renounce." In this case the idea may be that they renounce him by their lifestyle.

5-16. While it is perhaps desirable to consider the section that deals with specific matters related to the false teachers as an extended unit, for formatting purposes the subparagraphs (vv. 5-7, vv. 8-13, vv. 14-16) are being used in outlining the book.

5-7. Jude wants to remind his readers of various facts from the past, even though they fully know these truths. Jude's purpose is not to give new information but to motivate action. The idea of reminding is also important in 2 Peter. The importance of the adverbial modifying phrase, "once for all," has been variously understood; some translations connect the phrase with the verb "knowing" and others with the verb "saving."

"Lord" is a reference to YHWH, the one who delivered (*sozo*, to save, the word does not have a strictly spiritual emphasis here) the people from Egypt. Afterward, some of those who left Egypt were destroyed (*apollumi*, figuratively, to die, to perish) for their unbelief (see Hebrews 3-4 for an account of the same events).

The descriptions in vv. 6-7 are reminiscent of 2 Pet. 2:4-6. (See comments there.) Those who were delivered from Egypt worshiped God and later turned away. The angels are set forth as examples of those who after worshiping God later rebelled. The use of these two examples suggests that the false teachers were formerly believers. They turned grace into immorality. The angels Jude mentions are those who did not keep or maintain their own place in the order or rank, possibly referring to an order of authority. They left their own habitation for the great day of judgment. This description suggests that they had been assigned a place by God. What motivated them to leave their assigned role is not revealed. In the original text, the placement of the phrase "for the great day of judgment" is ambiguous. Were the angels anticipating the judgment day in their decision, or does God keep them unto the day of judgment? "These" God has kept in eternal chains in darkness. The repetition of the verb gives emphasis. When certain angels decided not to **keep** their appropriate roles and places, God placed them in eternal chains in darkness to **keep** them until the day of judgment. The reference to Tartarus in 2 Pet. 2:4 is not included in the text in Jude.

The judgment on the angels is like the judgment on Sodom and Gomorrah and the surrounding cities. A specific point of similarity ("same way") is the presence of immorality and unnatural desire (literally, "strange flesh"). "Strange (*heteros*, other) flesh" is apparently a reference to homosexuality, specifically mentioned in the Sodom and Gomorrah narrative in Genesis 19). Another point of similarity is the punishment of eternal fire. Jude uses these examples to warn his readers against the false teachers. The New Testament clearly speaks of eternal punishment; here that punishment is associated with eternal fire.

8-13. The false teachers are described with the use of several illustrations. Jude sees the false teachers as similar ("in the same way") to the rebellious examples he has just cited. The false teachers by dreaming contaminate the flesh, despite authority, and blaspheme or insult "glories." (See 2 Pet. 2:10-11 for a parallel to this passage and see comments there.) Perhaps the reference to "dreaming" refers to the fact that they claimed prophetic powers, or it may simply say that they claimed to receive information in visions. That their dreams were not valid revelations can be seen in the results. Immorality and rejection of authority are repeated from v. 4. To "blaspheme glories" is difficult to interpret, both in this verse and in the parallel in 2 Pet. 2:10. If Jude is citing Peter, the reference is best understood in the context of Peter's writings. I repeat the comment from 2 Pet. 2:10: "If the authority despised in v. 10a is the authority of Christ, insulting the 'glories' of Christ likely continues the same line of thought. Such would connect naturally with questioning Christ's authority."

Verse 9 is similar to 2 Pet. 2:11, except in the Jude text Michael is specifically mentioned whereas Peter mentions only angels generally. The principle is the same. The boldness of the false teachers who openly practice immorality, reject authority, and speak evil of "glories" is set in contrast to the caution of Michael the archangel. The dispute between Michael and Satan is part of Jewish tradition and is not mentioned elsewhere in Scripture. The point is not to affirm the validity of the Jewish tradition—the point is to use an illustration that was apparently well-known to Jude's readers to point out the arrogance of false teachers who would dare to pass judgments by rejecting authority and blaspheming those things to which God attaches glory. Michael did not dare to bring judgment but left the matter of rebuke in God's hands.

A parallel to v. 10 appears in 2 Pet. 2:12. The false teachers show no restraint and blaspheme things they do not understand. Blaspheme is repeated from v. 11: they blaspheme "glories." They do not understand the glory of the Lord. Michael and the angels would not dare blaspheme, but the false teachers are quick to speak evil, even of that which they do not understand. The false teachers are irrational, without understanding, no better than unthinking (*alogos*) animals, and in (by) these things they are destroyed (*phtheiro*, corrupted).

Verses 11-13 have many parallels and similarities with 2 Peter 2:12-16. Jude uses some of the same illustrations and same phrases as are used in 2 Peter. In v. 11, Jude's use of Balaam as an example of hasty speech is paralleled in 2 Peter. Jude mentions two others examples that are not mentioned in Peter, Cain (Gen. 4) and Korah (Num. 16), both of whom serve as examples of those whom God rejected because of a haughty spirit and their rejection of authorities.

The false teachers are as hidden reefs (*spilas*) posing unseen danger. The translation as blemishes (NIV, NRSV, KJV = spots) comes from *spilos*. These are two different words which vary in only one letter. The false teachers are present in the love feasts of the church. The parallel text in 2 Pet. 2:13 uses a verb form to describe feasting, but does not specifically mention love feasts. The love feasts were common meals shared by the early church, often with the Lord's Supper integrated into the shared meal, as would have been the case at the Passover. The false teachers feast fearlessly, caring *(poimaino)* for themselves. The verb means "to shepherd," thus they are like the shepherds who shepherd themselves (Ezek. 34).

The last descriptions in vv. 12-13 suggest promise without fulfillment (clouds without water, trees without fruit); chaos and uncontrolled, hidden desires (wild waves); and being directionless (wandering stars). 2 Pet. 2:17 mentions springs without water. At times, a tree partially dead with a minimal root system will produce some fruit. "Trees without fruit" pictures utter uselessness. The wild waves are "mists driven by the storm" in 2 Pet. 2:17. In Jude, the focus is not only on an inability to manage the impulses that drive human beings, but also on the shameful behavior that results. The verb form "to wander" (*planao*, related to our word planet) was used several times in 2 Peter. The texts of Jude and 2 Peter converge again in the final phrase: black darkness is reserved for such (cf. Jude 13, 2 Pet. 2:17b).

The Lord is coming with ten thousands and ten thousands of his holy ones, to execute judgment against all, to convict all the **ungodly** concerning all their **ungodly** works which they committed in an **ungodly** way, and concerning all the hard words which **ungodly** sinners spoke against him. --Jude 14b-15

14-16. In these three verses, Jude completes his description of the false teachers. The citation from Enoch, the seventh from Adam (Gen. 5) is from the apocalyptic book, *1 Enoch* (1:9). Jude's use of the verb, to prophesy (*propheteuo*), should not be understood to mean that he thought Enoch's work was inspired. The verb *propheteuo* was used in the first century in various ways with various meanings: to describe foretelling, of inspired writings, of speaking for another person, and of preaching. The citation from *1 Enoch* is found in Jude 14b-15. Jude's purpose in citing this extra-biblical text is to reinforce the certainty of judgment, convicting the ungodly of ungodly deeds done in ungodly ways, convicting ungodly sinners who spoke against the Lord. The Lord (YHWH) came with myriads of his saints (holy ones). This possibly refers to angelic beings. Both angels and saints will accompany Jesus at his return (1 Thess. 3:13; 2 Thess. 1:7).

In v. 15, the repetition of the word "ungodly" is noteworthy (see v. 4). The focus is on ungodliness and the ungodly ones who speak against (blaspheme) the Lord. The final description of the false teachers in v. 16 serves as a summary. These are grumblers, fault finders, walking according to their lusts, speaking exaggerations (*huperogkos*, swellings, thus the common translation, speaking arrogantly), flattering for their own gain. Some of these descriptions are similar to descriptions of the false teachers in 2 Peter 2.

17-23. After giving an extended description of the false teachers, Jude moves to warnings and exhortations. The presence of false teachers should not be a surprise. The apostles had predicted the coming of scoffers who would follow their own ungodly desires.

The repetition of the vocative term of address, "beloved," serves to begin a new section of text. The need to remember is repeated from verses 3 and 5. Jude appeals to the words of the apostles to support his admonition. The message of the apostles (the use of the imperfect verb tense suggests that it was a message repeated several times) predicted scoffers (*empaiktes*) in the last time. The word for scoffers appears only here and in 2 Pet. 3:3. Jude's use of this phrase shows that he thought of himself as living in the last time. The false teachers are further described as divisive line-drawers, carnal, and not having the Spirit.

Verses 20-23 serve as a contrast to verses 17-19. In verse 20, the vocative is repeated, "beloved." The text in vv. 20-23 is uncertain in some places, and in addition, it has a somewhat complex grammatical construction. Identifying the verb sequence in vv. 20-22 is a first step toward beginning an analysis of these verses: building up (present participle), praying (present participle), keep yourselves (aorist imperative), waiting (present participle), be merciful (imperative), save (imperative), be merciful (imperative), hating (participle).

The last three imperatives use the Greek particle "certainly" (*men*, truly, indeed) followed by two uses of the Greek particle "yet" (*de*, but, on the other hand). This construction ties the last three imperatives together. In these verses, the second and third imperatives serve to amplify the first member of the group. It is difficult to translate this construction into English without additional words. Here is a summary: Certainly (*men*) Christians should have mercy (first imperative) on those who waver; showing mercy will require both (*de*) saving (second imperative) some and (*de*) being merciful (third imperative) to others with reverence for God.

The participles are best understood as participles of means. The sentence can be outlined by using the imperatives. First, maintain yourself in God's love. How does one keep oneself in God's love? By edifying oneself, praying, and waiting. Second, be merciful to all of those who have been influenced by the false teachers, those who waver or doubt. This will be done through two actions: save those who have strayed so far as to be in danger of judgment, and be merciful to the rest with reverence. The final participle can be understood as modifying the last three imperatives. The reason Christians are merciful to those with doubts, the reason Christians work diligently to save those in danger of judgment, the reason Christians reverently extend mercy to one another, is their hatred of sin.

Here is what the teacher of truth will teach. Here is a description of genuine Christianity. By building up faith, and by praying in the Holy Spirit, Christians will stay in God's love, waiting for eternal life. The Christian will be merciful to all who doubt, to save those on the fringe by snatching them back from the fire, and to be merciful to all with reverence, hating the danger posed by the pollution of sin.

Mercy showed up unexpectedly in v. 1, here it repeated twice (vv. 22-23). The Christian is concerned about and responsible for self. The Christian is also concerned about those who are being influenced by the false teachers. In some cases, Christians can save those who have strayed. Jude uses the idea of saving something by snatching it from the fire. In the context, one may remember the fire of judgment (v. 7). Christians recognize the danger of contamination, especially visible in the ungodliness of the false teachers.

24-25. The book closes with a doxology rather than the typical closing salutation one would expect in a letter. These verses are one of the outstanding doxologies of the New Testament. They focus on God's glory, seen in what he does and what he will do.

Note the affirmations of verse 24.
- God is able. This phrase is used in three New Testament doxologies (Rom. 16:25, Eph. 3:20, Jude 24).
- To keep you free from falling.
- To make you stand in the presence of his glory.
- Blameless (without blemish).
- With rejoicing.

The doxology concludes in v. 25. The "one who is able" is identified as "only God." The parallelism is clear, as is the reference to monotheism. God is one. God is Savior. Jesus Christ is Lord. In the Old Testament, Lord was a reference to YHWH. Jesus Christ is the one through whom God's mercy and salvation comes.

"To him be glory, majesty, power, and authority, before all ages, now, and unto all ages." Glory refers to God's splendor. Majesty refers to God's greatness. Power refers to God's sovereignty. Authority refers to God's rule. God's nature is unchanging. The timelessness of eternity is described: before there was time, now, and forever.

www.ingramcontent.com/pod-product-compliance
Lightning Source LLC
Chambersburg PA
CBHW071525040426
42452CB00008B/898